DOES GOD SING?

DOES GOD SING?

A Musical Journey

Aaron Robinson

TATE PUBLISHING
AND ENTERPRISES, LLC

Does God Sing?
Copyright © 2012 by Aaron Robinson. All rights reserved.

No part of this publication may be reproduced, stored in a retrieval system or transmitted in any way by any means, electronic, mechanical, photocopy, recording or otherwise without the prior permission of the author except as provided by USA copyright law.

The opinions expressed by the author are not necessarily those of Tate Publishing, LLC.

Published by Tate Publishing & Enterprises, LLC
127 E. Trade Center Terrace | Mustang, Oklahoma 73064 USA
1.888.361.9473 | www.tatepublishing.com

Tate Publishing is committed to excellence in the publishing industry. The company reflects the philosophy established by the founders, based on Psalm 68:11,
"The Lord gave the word and great was the company of those who published it."

Book design copyright © 2012 by Tate Publishing, LLC. All rights reserved.
Cover design by Allen Jomoc
Interior design by Jomel Pepito

Published in the United States of America

ISBN: 978-1-62147-463-0
1. Religion / Christian Life / Inspirational
2. Biography & Autobiography / Composers & Musicians
13.05.10

Dedication

I dedicate this book to:

My Mother

Who all my life has sent me stories of inspiration during times of personal struggle.

Dr. Rev. Robert Dow

Who taught me how to believe in them.

Acknowledgements

Special thanks are given to the following

* * *

Broad Cove Community Church

Jeannette Chapman – Estelle Saastamoinen

* * *

Friendship United Methodist Church

Rev. Walter Brown

* * *

Immanuel Baptist Church

Dr. Rev. Peter and Judy Gray
Dr. Rev. Robert and Eleanor Dow
Dr. Thomas and Lois Verlee

* * *

*North Waldoboro Church
of the Nazarene*

Rev. Emery and Gertrude Pratt

*   *   *

Dr. Anthony Antolini – Ms. Ellen Chickering

Mr. Paul Havenstein II
"The Crazy Organist"

*   *   *

Ervin and Jean Robinson
George and Karen Bruns

*Without whose loving kindness and generosity
this book would have never been written*

Harmony Haven, Saco Maine, 2009

Table of Contents

Preface 11
All Music Comes from God 13
It Is Well with My Soul 21
Was that Jesus? 27
Keep the Channel Open 39
God Stomping through the Sanctuary 49
Sing with Life! 55
Murodhon 71
His Eye Is on the Sparrow 79
Precious Lord, Take My Hand 89
Crossing to the Other Side 99
The Tuning Fork 115
The Healing Power of Music 139
The Song of the Crane 163
The Poetry of the Earth 169
Epilogue 177
Bibliography 179

Preface

Throughout my life I have been blessed with constant reminders that music is the most powerful and natural of all art forms. It is created without our having to produce it. We are surrounded by it. It envelops us and flows through us.

If you are spiritual in any way, music has the ability to cause a profound reaction within you that can easily change the mood you're in, or more dramatically, change your outlook on a particular situation or even completely change your life.

I personally choose in these moments of divine musical revelation to see these happenings as valuable lessons for a better life—God singing to me. If I listen, I can sing along. If I listen hard enough and long enough and learn the tune well enough, I may even be able to sing it to others.

If I should die, God forbid,
let this be my epitaph,

*The only proof he needed for
the existence of God was music.*

—Kurt Vonnegut

All Music Comes from God

When I was sixteen years old I was invited to become the organist for two churches in the Midcoast area on the Coast of Maine: the Broad Cove Church in Cushing and the Methodist Church in Friendship. They were sister churches and shared not only an organist but a pastor, as well.

Every Sunday morning it was customary for me to play for the 9:30 a.m. service in Cushing and then quickly drive along the back roads to Friendship and play for their 11 a.m. service some ten minutes away (twenty if it was wintertime). I was fortunate in many ways to start my musical career in such a quaint area that was filled with history and charm–Cushing in particular.

In this small village, there was a tiny post office, a single corner general store, and the Broad Cove church. That was it.

However, this did not limit its many historical claims. For instance, the South Cushing Baptist Church, which no longer holds services, was frequented by brother and sister Christina and Alvaro Olson who were immortalized by painter Andrew Wyeth (a frequent resident of Cushing) in many portraits, including his most famous work: *Christina's World.*

Although both Christina and Alvaro had passed away several years before my arrival, the town knew well of the Olson family and the Wyeths. In fact, the Olson house still stands today just along Hathorn Point Road. I was even fortunate enough to meet Andy and his wife Betsy (a very kind and gentle person) on occasion during their visits.

To add to this, an elderly lady, whom I respectfully called Mrs. Gowing, regularly attended the Cushing church during my early years as organist and told me stories of how her grandmother once sat upon the knee of Louis Moreau Gottschalk (the famous nineteenth-century American composer and pianist) while he made a mouse dance from underneath a handkerchief for her amusement.

Mrs. Gowing was a tiny, elegant lady for whom I would play the piano music of Gottschalk in tribute to her grandmother and to her great delight. I would play *The Dying Poet*, *The Last Hope* (from which the melody leant itself to the evening hymn "Holy Ghost, With Light Divine") and on special, patriotic Sundays, *The Union.*

In fact, the very piano on which I played these pieces had been donated by a couple "from away" who summered in Cushing and attended the little church and who had once lived next door to Peter Wilhousky, the legendary choral arranger who set the famous "Battle Hymn of the Republic." Each summer on the

Does God Sing?

Fourth of July I would play my own rendition of this piece for solo piano; it became a tradition. Many pieces that I played became traditions throughout the church year—only because I was still quite young and very limited in my knowledge of music literature.

I was lucky in more ways than one. The organist job at the Cushing church was not only my first introduction into the world of church music but any form of public performance, as well. I had just started playing the piano the year before, and although I was self-taught, I quickly rose to performing at a level that would meet conservatory standards.

Even though the organ was not an instrument I would master for some twenty years, the time spent in Cushing and Friendship offered me a chance to experiment and learn the instrument as a young aspiring musician should—in a safe, accepting environment. Because of this, I was able to share my gifts and talents with my first attentive, appreciative, and certainly *forgiving* "audience"—the congregation.

I had no formal training of any kind, and I certainly lacked all knowledge of sacred music appropriate for a church worship service. Those years in Cushing supplied me with the opportunity to mold and shape each stage of my exposure to the world of music—both sacred and secular. But this also had its limits.

Every new piece I learned, no matter what it was or who it was by, I was eager to share it with my church family the following Sunday. At first it started out innocently with various classical pieces that ever so slightly stretched the boundaries of what was considered proper and suitable for a Sunday morning service, especially in a small village church on the coast of Maine.

Decades later I would be introduced to the large, inner-city church life that had inherited "performance" organ literature thanks to the eccentric personalities of Virgil Fox, Diane Bish, and many of their devoted followers. It was acceptable (and almost expected) for an accomplished, highly paid organist to play Charles Widor's *Toccata* from his fifth Organ Symphony on Easter Sunday or even the monumental *Variations on 'America'* by Ives.

So, when I started to bridge the gap between Bach and Brahms, Tchaikovsky and Debussy, Satie and Elgar, Gottschalk and Gershwin, and then proceeded to condense all composers to certain eras, nationalities and styles of music, something had to give—which it did.

Without question, I could get away with playing Sir Edward Elgar's *Pomp and Circumstance* each June for the graduating class. Maybe even a grand, sweeping version of the "Anniversary Waltz" by Russian composer Ivanovici for a couple in the congregation honoring fifty years of marriage. This was deemed admissible within the house of the Lord since it celebrated the joys and blessings of life.

But when I had at last reached the doors of the Broadway stage and innocently performed a medley by Rodgers and Hammerstein because it ended with the majestic finale "You'll Never Walk Alone" (by way of such sacred classics as "Oh, What a Beautiful Morning" and "I'm Gonna Wash That Man Right Out of My Hair"), it was time to have a little chat.

I can remember vividly the pastor that morning, sitting next to me, turning my pages, leaning in close and whispering, "I think this should be the last number."

But I hadn't even come to the grand finale yet!

After the service he took me aside very kindly and with great compassion and quietly educated me in the correct way to choose appropriate music for a church service. "This is Broad *Cove,* not Broad*way,*" he said with a touch of serious humor. "Let's try and stick with a more sacred, classical format for right now. We'll leave the concert stage for another time, okay?"

Oddly enough, in the years that followed this episode, he became the most loyal of supporters for my philosophy of sharing all styles of music within a worship service and even asked if I would play certain pieces that I had become well-known for throughout my years as a concert pianist and Broadway musical director, including George Gershwin's *Rhapsody in Blue* and "Memory" from the musical *Cats* because he and his wife had just returned from seeing the show in New York (which they *loved*), and he had the desire to preach a sermon based on the song's message.

But that was later—this was now. I had to face a rather humiliating realization by way of a delicate but rather important lesson: *church was no place for secular music.* However, all this would change one day, due in part to a very significant person in my life: Estelle Saastamoinen.

Estelle was a short, spunky, powerhouse of a woman with a loud voice, thick with the accent and drive of a coastal Maine local. She spoke her mind frequently but was never mean-spirited, brash, or offensive in any way. Her words were direct and to the point based on what she believed to be right and true.

Within weeks of my arrival Estelle and I developed a very special friendship, and she watched over me as would any self-adopted grandmother. We even had a secret Sunday morning ritual.

Every Sunday morning I would arrive at seven thirty to practice whatever music I had chosen to perform for that morning's worship service. Like clockwork, Jeannette Chapman (a devoted member of the church) would arrive shortly after me to turn on the heat and make sure everything was up and running before congregation members started to gather.

During my practice Jeannette would poke her head in from the side room and say with a bright smile and a chipper voice, "That sounds wonderful!" This was when I was still in my Chopin and Mozart years.

Then, after Jeannette would make her rounds and head back home to get ready for church, Estelle would pull into the church parking lot. I could hear her shut the car door with her usual force and make her way up the walk with great purpose and throw open the door to the narthex.

She would come in from the back and sit in her normal seat—three pews down, on the left, directly in the middle (which was partitioned in the box-style fashion of small, coastal Maine churches). Plunking herself down with an exhaled breath, she would rest her arms on top of the pew and lean back. Never once did she interrupt me or say even a word while I practiced. She came only to listen.

As was our usual custom at the end of my practice time I would turn to Estelle, and she would always say the same words no matter what I played, "Yea'uh, that was good. I liked that…" This went on for years.

Then came the fateful show tunes and secular period of my tenure as organist. Based on the fact that *there is nothing like a dame*, word got around quickly that maybe I was not right for this job anymore. After the pastor had a word with me, I began to think the same thing. So I reined in my selections almost to a screeching halt.

Then one Sunday I was playing *Sheep May Safely Graze* by Bach and the *Adagio* from Mozart's *Clarinet Concerto*. At the close of the second, I turned to Estelle for her usual approval—but to my astonishment, she did not offer it. This time was different.

Instead, she spoke the most profound and encouraging words that I would ever hear—words that would set my life in music on a completely different path from that day forward.

"Don't let 'em tell ya what'cha can or can't play." Estelle said firmly, "Play what'cha want … all music comes from God."

All music comes from God…

Those five simple words, spoken by a small, spitfire of a lady would change my life forever.

Aaron Robinson

Estelle is gone now. She passed some years later. But her words have forever stayed with me. The window was thrown open that day, and it has never been shut since. It can't be shut…because she was right. All music *does* come from God.

Thank you Estelle.

It Is Well with My Soul

It always amazes me when I read stories of inspiration and the music that is created by it. Some of the most beautiful melodic strains ever written have been composed in the presence of God.

Take for instance composer George Frederic Handel. While composing his masterpiece *Messiah* in a small London house on Brook Street, the great master of choral music wrote, "I did think I did see all Heaven before me, and the great God Himself." (He had just finished writing the celebrated *Hallelujah Chorus*.) What's more, as legend states, the mighty affirmation of the music was so great that King George I rose to his feet at an early performance of the Oratorio.

* * *

I can remember the exact moment when I knew that God had the ability to reveal Himself through music. It was such an overpowering, spiritual experience that I knew right then and there that I would devote my life to music. Whether to praise Him directly or to be used as a channel for His divine glory, by inspiring others through my gifts and talents, I felt as though I had "seen all Heaven before me" when at the impressionable age of eleven I first heard the hymn "It Is Well with My Soul."

Now this was no ordinary revelation or mere awakening to God's mighty presence and the power that music could have over a person. The setting in which it occurred was just as influential as the music itself. I could not simply have listened to this beautiful hymn on a record player or radio. It had to come from the human body by way of the voice raised in song—and many.

To give you some personal background, I was raised in the Nazarene church and lived in a remote, backwoods part of town that was independent enough to have its own small, country church—similar to the hundreds that can still be found all over New England even today. Although long torn down and gone now, I can remember it just as if it was yesterday.

The church itself was a basic, simple structure. The walls of which were made of large, hand-sawn planks. One could, at times, actually see through the slits between the boards and into the surrounding woods outside. A grange hall sat directly across the road where church suppers were held—an old building that had a large wood stove in the center of the long hall that reached the ceiling, where it was then divided off into large ducts that ran the length of the room in all directions. The floors were worn, slat-wood floors.

Does God Sing?

The church had a modest pulpit, an old upright piano in the left front corner, and hard wooden pews that were filled every Sunday morning, Sunday evening, Tuesday evening, Wednesday evening, and sometimes Saturday. (God bless the Nazarenes!) The congregation was largely made up of families from the adjoining towns: north, south, east, and west. It was in this crude structure of a church that music changed my life forever.

* * *

A prominent, respected "Brother" of the church had died—Emery Pratt, an elderly minister who had devoted his life to God and the church. My family knew both him and his wife, Gertrude, very well. In fact, since we lived right next door, we grew up calling them Grammy and Grampy Pratt.

I never knew the impact this man's life had on so many people until the day I was brought to the little church in the backwoods and saw for the first time the pews packed elbow to elbow, end to end with people. The sides and back walls were lined with respectful gatherers who chose to stand once all the seats had been filled. Oh! So many people! I was lost in a sea of people when I sat down.

I was intimidated, as much as any eleven-year-old boy could be, by all those esteemed figures of faith that had assembled to praise and remember the life of this great man. So it was no wonder that I sat in complete silence throughout many of the testimonies that poured forth – Brother after Brother, Sister after Sister. It grew hot in that little church, and I grew tired. It was then...

suddenly…a gentleman stood up and announced that we would now be singing Brother Pratt's favorite hymn, "It Is Well with My Soul."

I had never heard this hymn before, but I can tell you my entire body came alive, and the hairs on my little head stood on end when I heard the immense sound of those full, glorious chords emanating from all those people. It was indescribable.

The Sacred Harp singers of Alabama have a special place for the "leader" who cues the singing from a center position, which is surrounded by the four parts in their sections. It is called the "sacred square," and it is where all the sound in the world hits you with such a force that your whole body vibrates—*literally* vibrates. It was this similar effect that I felt when those around me began singing in four-part harmony, "When peace, like a river, attendeth my way; when sorrows like sea billows roll…"

I had never heard four-part harmony before in my life and certainly not *a cappella*. So to then hear the magnificent chorus begin with the unison statement, "It is well …" followed by the response, "It is well…" in such rich yet simple tones, it brought forth tears for a reason that I could not explain at such a young age.

I couldn't help but cry. The tears just came, and I felt tingly all over, and my body became electrifyingly warm inside. Every fiber of my being responded to this sound, and from that moment on I knew the immense power music could have over a person's mind and body—and the spiritual impact it was capable of producing in one's soul.

Does God Sing?

* * *

One would think that to write such an inspiring hymn, a person would have to be not only happy but also content, blessed, and certainly at peace. Yet these distressed words, "When sorrows like sea billows roll," were not written by such an individual. Just the opposite, they were penned by a man who had endured unthinkable tragedy.

In the mid 1800s, times were good for Horatio G. Spafford, a successful Chicago lawyer, and his wife, Anna. They were blessed with a loving family, a strong, fulfilling marriage, and a deeply shared passion in their faith. However, in 1870 things started to take a turn for the worse.

At the age of four, the Spaffords' only son died of scarlet fever. In addition to this devastating loss, Spafford had invested significantly in real estate along the shores of Lake Michigan. A year later in 1871 every last one of these properties was to be razed by the great Chicago Fire. It was then that Spafford decided to take his wife and four daughters to England in hopes of separating them from the disasters that had recently befallen them.

Traveling to New York, the Spafford family was scheduled to board the *Ville de Havre*—a French ocean liner bound for Britain. Yet just before they were to set sail, a delay forced Horatio to stay behind. Wishing to not spoil the vacation, Spafford convinced his wife to go as planned and that he would follow at a later time.

Having agreed, Mrs. Spafford and her four daughters sailed on toward England while Spafford returned to Chicago. Within just nine days, however, he received a telegram from his wife, which read, "Saved alone."

On November 2, 1873, the *Ville de Havre* had collided with an English vessel, the *Lochearn*. It sank in just twelve minutes and claimed the lives of 226 people—including Spafford's four daughters. Anna had been saved only by a floating plank, which supported her unconscious body.

Grief stricken, Horatio Spafford boarded the next ship departing from New York to unite with his bereaved wife. During the voyage the ship's captain had called Spafford to the bridge and said, "A careful reckoning has been made, and I believe we are now passing the place where the *de Havre* was wrecked. The water is three miles deep."

It was at that precise moment that Spafford returned to his cabin below and penned the words of his great hymn, taken from 2 Kings 4:26. "…though her soul is vexed within her, she still maintains that 'It is well'…"

Later, Spafford's words would inspire composer Philip Bliss to set the text to music. A hymn that would, some hundred years later, inspire a young boy of eleven years, sitting in a backwoods Nazarene church, his face wet with tears, to devote his life to music.

Was that Jesus?

Growing up in the Nazarene church, the question of, "Was that Jesus?" was placed in my head at a very early age and continued to rework itself throughout the many sermons, children's stories, and Sunday school lessons that I heard.

I could not comprehend at the time what exactly a "metaphor" was, so the message supporting this concept was lost on my young mind. I was literally trying to *see* Jesus.

The idea behind the familiar story of a car broken down by the side of the road, its driver stranded with no help in sight when suddenly a stranger stops to lend a hand, blew my young mind.

Hearing the final testimony: "I don't know where he came from or even his name, but before I could turn and thank him, he was gone." "Was that Jesus?" just furthered the confusion.

What did it matter? I thought. *Jesus was driving a car! How cool is that!*

When, as I grew older, the stories developed into more graphic details and scenarios, I began to question.

It wasn't the idea of the homeless person on the street who approaches you for change so that they can "get a hot meal" that I couldn't grasp; it was the moral that was driven home in an attempt to make the separation between being a good Samaritan and such unsympathetic statements of reply as: "Sorry, I can't be bothered to stop," or "Hey, buddy, I made my way. You make yours."

What was going on here? First Jesus is driving around in his car helping people, and a few Sundays later he's homeless? What happened? Couldn't he afford the payments? And what's more, if this homeless person was indeed Jesus, why *wouldn't* you want to stop and help him?

Even when livestock was incorporated, it still complicated things for me.

Take the familiar story of the sheep and the goats: "…But, Lord? When were you sick? When were you in prison? When were you hungry or without clothes?… Tell us, Lord. Tell us."

Looking around at the faces of the congregation, I attempted to categorize the people in terms of sheep and goats.

"Okay," I would say, "the sweet, little old man sitting three pews back and to the left who always gives me candy and a smile, he's *got* to be a sheep. But his bitter, old, white-haired, sallow-faced wife that always stands up and complains during meetings—she's *definitely* a goat. She even has a little beard to prove it."

Well, I must say that over time I finally made the connection between metaphor and moral. Further still, now that I am an adult and can see doing what is right in retrospect, I realize that at certain times in my life I have been more goat than sheep.

Even though it was more a part of my character in my early twenties than in my later adult years, there are still times even today when I find myself saying, "I can't be bothered now"—a great tune by Gershwin but certainly not a motto by which to live one's life.

However, it is a lesson that must be *learned*, unfortunately, and the two sides of this lesson-coin are bitter and sweet. It is only through missed opportunities and poorly chosen paths that we then discover all the blessings that we missed all on account of our asking, "…Was that Jesus?" When the question really should be, "…*Is* this Jesus?"

> "Then He will answer them, saying, 'For as much as you did not do this for the least of my brethren, you did not do this for me'" (Matthew 25:45).

Let me tell you a story that happened to me when I was just starting my musical career.

* * *

Many concert pianists will claim that they started their formal training at a very early age. This was not the case when it came to my life. Even though in my late teens I was giving solo concerts, I had only been playing the piano for little over a year, and quickly became known and even reviewed as somewhat of a "wunderkind" from both sides of the tracks who was able to play the most difficult pieces from not only the classical repertoire but also the popular, secular works for the piano, as well. From Rachmaninoff to Gershwin, Brahms to Joplin, Mozart to Morton—I played them all.

But newly found fame can be both a blessing and a curse.

If one is told repeatedly by enough people that they are a "genius" (especially as a teenager), one starts to believe it. So it is no wonder that when I was hired to play, direct, and conduct at an early age it was this now-realized, self-inflated awareness of quality and talent that accompanied me.

I made mistakes. I burned bridges. I almost destroyed all that I had accomplished on account of that awareness. But in my defense in looking back, it was unintentional. (Although many people much older than I would look upon me, form an opinion, and say, "He knows what he's doing.")

But I learned from my mistakes (the bitter side of the lesson-coin). In fact, I'm still learning today. I believe we all have the ability (and a "charge to keep" – as the familiar hymn states) to learn something new all the time. To not only learn from our mistakes but also grow on account of the learning.

Until the day comes when we are unable to learn anymore, my motto remains, "A good teacher never stops learning." And so my "life lessons" started hand in hand with my talent and fame.

* * *

Does God Sing?

Through mutual friends I was introduced to a coffee shop owner in the city who became interested in hiring me to play for a few hours each Sunday afternoon. I would be expected to take requests, and although there was a small stipend, tips were an essential part of the job.

With this in mind, I played what I thought the people wanted to hear and certainly played what they requested. They were happy, and so I was happy. Life was good.

But something became a constant on these Sunday afternoon performances that inhibited this happiness—a constant annoyance.

It was winter when I first began playing at the coffee shop—a time when the homeless made a routine of wandering the city. Much like on a schedule they would stop into certain establishments for just the appropriate amount of time in order to get warm, perhaps receive a handout, and leave before the owner moved them along and out the door. It was a ritual that I understood but certainly did not accept when it interfered with my duties—and performing.

I played on a concert upright—a fairly good instrument for its make, and it could handle all styles of music. Because of this featured ability, I required a certain amount of attention and a proper level of quiet when I was playing in order to create an effect. So you could expect my reaction when a weatherworn, rather loud, and certainly intrusive, foul-smelling, "bum" came through the door one Sunday afternoon.

If he had simply gone up to the counter and lingered there, or even sat down at a table, I wouldn't have minded. I felt it was the proprietor's duty to deal with the homeless; it was not my business. But that wasn't the case in this situation. He immediately strolled over to the piano and leaned heavily against it.

Watching my hands, the homeless man would make comments and sometimes even sing along to the melodies I played. All the while filling my nostrils with the most repugnant smells of wet body odor and greasy, dirty clothes. He was a complete offense in every way to all my senses: mind, body, and soul.

As time went on and Sundays passed, I began to grow increasingly anxious just waiting for the bells to ring from atop the door. Catching the waft of the all-too-familiar, unpleasant smell from the street winds blowing in the arrival of this homeless man, I knew my happiness was over. I would be plagued for the rest of the afternoon.

Like a bad recurring nightmare, it was the same routine. Like clockwork, he would enter, shout, "Hello!" in a very loud voice, greet certain faces he recognized, buy a small cup of hot, strong, black coffee, and tip his dirty hat to Abe, the owner. It would only take a few seconds at most for him to do all this before making his way over to my piano.

From the change gathered on the street, he would have just enough for a small cup of coffee while the rest (mostly pennies) would be scattered on top of the piano with the request that I play something by Hoagy Carmichael. No other composer—it always had to be Hoagy Carmichael.

Does God Sing?

No matter what song I played by this great American songwriter, he knew and would never hesitate to sing along in a rowdy, booming voice, "Georgia on My Mind," "Lazy Bones," "Stardust." Before long, I not only grew impatient but resentful. *Carmichael is one of my favorite composers of all time,* I thought, *and this man is ruining his music for me!*

Soon I realized that the only hope of ridding myself of this man and regain some sort of contentment was to say (true or not) that I did not know any more tunes by Hoagy Carmichael. *It was the only way,* I thought. So I set the date; the very next Sunday would be the last time I would indulge him.

Sunday came, and so did he—change in hand. The familiar greetings, the unpleasant odor, the cup of strong black coffee, and the dirty, cold pennies slammed down on top of the piano. He had already become too familiar in his manner of request. "Play something by Hoagy Carmichael," he'd bellow as if it were an order.

I turned slowly and spoke the most words I'd ever uttered to him, "I'm sorry, but I do not know anymore Carmichael tunes. I'm sorry."

To say whether or not he was shocked, disappointed, or even hurt is impossible for me to recall now. All I know is he stood there for some time…in silence. I played continuously from song to song without stopping so that he could not suggest a title during any pauses. He didn't know what to do except drink his coffee and leave.

I couldn't believe it. Was that it? Had I actually won this battle? Would I at last be rid of this man for good, or would he come in the very next Sunday with another composer and a whole slew of new requests? Only time would tell.

The following week, I was on edge. The hours ticked by, and yet the door did not ring out its bell and allow the street wind to blow in my weekly intruder. I *had* won. Finally, I could play in peace and not be bothered anymore.

Time passed, and so did the season. At the end, the coffee shop closed, unfortunately. The owners were relocating. On my last afternoon, I gathered my tips from the glass atop the piano and proceeded to go to the owner for my additional pay. We chatted for a while, and he thanked me for a job well done.

As was the custom, he gave me the compliments from the patrons that did not approach me personally. I was grateful and certainly happy. I thanked him for the opportunity. However, just before leaving, almost as a second thought, I turned and asked, "Say, do you remember that homeless guy who would come in each week and stand by the piano?"

"Who, Joe Johnson?" he said, "Oh, sure. He's been coming in here for as long as I can remember. Started back when the shop was down in the village." He paused for a moment then shook his head as though in fond remembrance, "Gosh, that was nearly twenty years ago now. Poor, old Joe."

"Poor, old Joe?" I asked. "Why? Because he's homeless?"

"Homeless?" he said. "Joe's been homeless for years. No, because he's dead. Died a few days ago, in fact."

Does God Sing?

My heart sank. I knew I wanted this man to go away, but never did I wish him dead. I couldn't help but feel guilty even though I knew it was foolish of me to think that I had any part in his death. He was old and homeless. It was just his time. All I could say was, "Gee, I'm sorry to hear that."

"Yup, Joe was a character, that's for sure," he continued. "Shame, though, he ended up that way. He once was a very important man—worked in Hollywood, you know."

"No, I didn't," I replied. How could I? I never asked. But now I was very much interested.

"He was in the film business—knew everybody. He was a music promoter and traveled around with many of the greats. Harry James, Benny Goodman…" And then he spoke the words that would stay with me forever. "But Hoagy Carmichael was his favorite. Oh, the stories he would tell!"

Once again, he became silent as though thinking of all those stories. This time, though, a warm, sweet smile came across his face. My face, on the other hand, flushed red. I felt sick and ashamed.

Here I was, just a kid—a cocky, stupid, egotistical kid—thinking I knew everything about anything. Little did I know that standing right next to me while I played the piano was a man who knew Harold Arlen, Cole Porter, Vernon Duke…and, of course, Hoagy Carmichael.

If only I had known, I would have talked with this man for hours after my shift regardless of his odor or boisterous conduct. I was *starved* for contact like that since growing up in a small town in Maine I could only read in books about the composers and songwriters whose works I played.

Was this Jesus?—of course not, just like it was never Jesus who actually stopped to help the stranded man on the side of the road with his broken-down car. But was the moral message that Jesus taught represented through this "bum?" Absolutely. Was God trying to sing to me through a homeless man—the least of my brethren—in a coffee shop? Without a doubt.

But I chose to close my ears, and I'll never get that chance again. I didn't even save the pennies. I would leave them there. I was too proud to pick them up and too "clean" to even touch them. Now I have a stain that can never be removed but stands as a reminder that God has given me a great gift that has the power to bring people into my life and change it forever.

I learned a valuable lesson that day. A lesson that has stuck with me and probably will remain with me for as long as I live. I let my judgment cloud my acceptance. I was so busy pointing out all the things I disliked about someone else I never realized that I was actually pointing out all my own flaws in the process: arrogance, impatience, pride, indifference.

* * *

A very wise man of faith by the name of Rev. Walter Brown once preached the following story, and I've never forgotten it.

Does God Sing?

Have you ever noticed what happens when you physically point a finger at someone? Do it now. Point your index finger as you would in making an argument to show someone else that they're wrong. You point your finger in the direction of that person, don't you? But what do you do with the other fingers? Where are they pointing?

Well, three of them are actually pointing back at you. Do you see?

Yet what do we do? We try to hide them. We cover them up with our thumb that we conveniently fold down over them.

Always remember that whenever you point out one single flaw in another, you're actually revealing three times as many in yourself.

Keep the Channel Open

While studying composition at the Boston Conservatory of Music in the early 1990s, I attended one of my first "contemporary" concerts. Up to this time in my life all the music I heard was self-introduced. Growing up in a small town in Maine, the only education I received came from reading, playing, and listening. I taught myself how to play the piano and organ, began composing my own music shortly thereafter, and any repertoire I was familiar with came from satisfying the deep desire to get my hands on as much music as I could possibly listen to or study.

The more understandable music of the great Russians opened up the world to the more emotional European composers, which lead to a small door that allowed just a taste of analytical compositions to filter through into my quickly expanding musical world. However, it would take several years before I could truly and honestly appreciate the celestial qualities of Johannes Brahms, the immensity of Gustav Mahler, or even the ingenious mathematical structure of the great

Johann Sebastian Bach. So to hear works by Elliot Carter, Milton Babbitt, and Steve Reich at such an early stage was anything but "part of the process."

As I sat in the concert hall, listening to atonal, serial music being performed, I would come to a realization through my disgust:

What I couldn't understand, I didn't like…

(There's a whole world in just that one statement. Not just relating to music, but to life in general. But for now, let's stick with music.)

Note after note hit me like a hammer for well over an hour until I almost couldn't stand it anymore. I turned to a classmate of mine and asked, "Is this *music?*"

With that question I resolved to leave after the very next piece. I didn't care whether my professors were displeased with my protest; I was not going to sit there one minute longer. Looking at the program, I saw the next piece—Steve Reich's *Piano Phase* for two pianos. For this I had to stay, since one of my professors was performing with the Conservatory's staff accompanist. I thought to myself, *How long could this actually be? It's minimalist music…a few notes and it's over. Right?*

Wrong!

The piece started with one pianist playing just five notes in a series that looped into a patterned melody of ten before starting over again. It was perpetual in motion and steady in tempo. Over and over again, the pianist played the same five notes—but then the second pianist began to play the same five notes in exact form and register. Two pianos playing the same ten note pattern seamlessly…endlessly. I wanted to shoot myself.

One minute turned into two. Two turned into three. I looked at the duration of the piece in the program, and it said, *"23 minutes."* Oh, dear Lord, when would this end? What did it *mean*? Why would anyone write such a piece?

I sat patiently with my eye on the door when all of a sudden something began to happen. The second pianist started to accelerate his tempo—but by just a fraction—while the first pianist remained constant. The notes started to separate, and it took a keen ear to hear that what was being produced was a live "reverb" effect. *Interesting,* I thought. *Okay, I'll stick with it for a few more minutes.*

As the music progressed, so did the second pianist. Slowly he moved steadily ahead in tempo. Not so that he was simply playing the piece faster, but in order to catch a new tempo, and thus a new rhythm of notes playing against the other pianist. From this, a whole world opened up. New melodies were formed, intricate rhythms started emerging, and just the slightest accent on a repeated note would create a pulsing drive that pulled you into the music deeper and deeper.

Before long the two pianists had stretched their overlapping series of notes to the point where they were completely opposite in their playing. Ten minutes in, and I hadn't even checked my watch. By this time I found myself leaning forward, mesmerized by what I was hearing, completely submerged in the sounds I was experiencing. How could this be?—and from just five notes? I was enthralled.

Upon first hearing, this music struck me like a tuning fork, and my first reaction was to shout, "No!"—but then a window of acceptance was opened and allowed me to respond in such a way that, while I didn't understand the mechanics of this piece, I *felt* the connection it was making with me.

Halfway through *Piano Phase* the second pianist started to slow his tempo—reversing his path, finding new rhythms, new melodies, until at last after twenty-three minutes the two pianists settled back into perfect unison. The performance ended with the first pianist playing alone the simple ten-note pattern he had started earlier.

The applause began, but I was too stunned to join in the acclamation. I *had* to know what had just happened. It wasn't until the following Monday, during my private composition time with my professor (the same one who had performed *Piano Phase* the Friday night before) that I was able to ask all the questions that had been swimming around in my brain over the weekend.

He didn't have the score with him, but he did show me the pattern on the piano. Three notes in his left hand on the white keys just above middle C: E–B–D and two notes in his right directly atop his left: F-sharp–C-sharp. He started the rhythmic pattern and showed me how it looped itself backward to form the ten-note melody. What I was seeing didn't match in my head what I was hearing. I didn't understand it, I couldn't explain it, but I was fascinated by it.

"Hadn't you ever heard music like that before?" my professor asked.

"Well, no," I said.

"I guess then you've never heard *Metamorphosis* by Philip Glass?"

"No, I haven't," I replied. "Should I?"

"Not particularly," my professor responded. "The performance doesn't matter. The principle of the piece does. You see, in this work, even though it is called 'Metamorphosis,' the music doesn't change—you do."

Wow! It was as if a light came on inside my head. I got it! I understood! And it made me feel all flush and warm inside. It inspired me. It proved that one did not need to understand to accept, and furthermore, no fresh air can enter a room through a closed window.

* * *

Nearly a decade later it was my turn to be on the other end of this setting. In one of my last appearances at the Round Top Center for the Performing Arts, I scheduled a lengthy program of all the pieces that had made my name known throughout the area as one associated with early Jazz and Ragtime. So lengthy was the program, in fact, that even my own father commented days later, "It was good—but a little too long."

A week later, the father of one of my students came into my studio to congratulate me on the concert. He confessed, however, that he had not intended to come and hear me play. In fact, his wife physically forced him to attend that night.

"I did *not* want to be there," the man stated.

Uncomfortable, I laughed. "I'm sorry."

"No need to apologize," he responded. "It wasn't you. I had so much work to do, I just wasn't in the mood to sit for two hours and listen to ragtime on a Saturday night."

"Well, I can understand that," I admitted.

"But I wanted to tell you," he said, sitting down and motioning with his hands for emphasis, "just as you were playing the last few selections, I turned to my wife and said, 'I'll wait for you in the car.'"

At this I laughed again, but he continued, "...and then you played your *Bluet Rag*. It was that one piece, so calm and peaceful, that I sat, began to relax, and just listened. I forgot all about my work and the stress of the week and listened. The music was so beautiful I didn't want it to end. I could have stayed there all night listening to that one piece."

I was touched. But I knew exactly what he was saying and what it implied: I had been a "channel of music."

What this man did not know was that I had to force myself to program that piece for the concert. So many people came to hear hard ragtime and fast jazz. They wanted Jelly Roll Morton and *12th Street Rag*, not Louis Chauvin and *Weeping Willow*. I programmed that piece for myself—not the audience. Little did I know it would have such an effect on the most resilient of audience members that evening.

In a letter to Agnes DeMille, Martha Graham writes,

> There is a vitality, a life force, an energy, a quickening that is translated through you into action, and because there is only one of you in all

of time this expression is unique. And if you block it, it will never exist through any other medium and will be lost. The world will not have it. It is not your business to determine how good it is, nor how valuable, nor how it compares with other expressions. It is your business to keep it yours clearly and directly, to stay open and aware to the urges that motivate you.

Keep the channel open....

* * *

Several years later, I found myself returning to the same area for a guest appearance. Again, many came to hear what I was famous for, and I didn't disappoint. *Dizzy Fingers* by Zez Confrey, *Handful of Keys* by "Fats" Waller, *Maple Leaf Rag* by Scott Joplin. But then I performed a rather unconventional piece for an encore, *Dance of the Blessed Spirits* by Christoph Willibald Gluck. I didn't play it for the audience, I played it for me; and in doing so allowed myself to give *and* receive at the same time.

But what I didn't expect was what happened after the concert. Waiting inconspicuously off to the side, as humbling praise was heaped upon me by a crowd of smiling audience members glowing with the joyous sounds of stride piano, a lady approached me amidst the gathering of fans.

"I wanted to thank you for the Gluck," she said, quietly.

"Oh," I said, surprised. "I'm glad you liked it."

"Actually, it's more than that," she said and began to tell her story. "I came here with my mother who has been a fan of yours for years. I'm just up visiting and had never heard you before tonight. Ragtime isn't really my music of choice, but I came to be with her."

She held fast to my hand as she spoke. "You're very talented. I enjoyed what I heard. But when you played the Gluck, something happened that left me a little skeptical, even now."

Continuing, she said, "I'm not much of a believer in what is considered to be what they call *metaphysical* or *other worldly*. In fact, I'm not very religious or even spiritual. (The concert had been held in a church.) But when you started playing, I saw what I guess some would call an aura form around you."

I began to be extremely taken by what this woman was relating to me.

"It was a brilliant, warm yellow that just surrounded you all over. I turned to my mother and said, 'Do you see that?'"

The mother, who had been standing nearby during this time, had come closer to listen to her daughter's story. "That's right," she confirmed. "She did! But I didn't know what she was talking about."

"I couldn't believe what I was seeing," the lady went on to say. "I tried to explain it to my mother, but she couldn't see it. So I just watched as you played. When you segued from the opening minuet to the minor melody, the aura grew brighter and changed from yellow to a deep orange. It filled the stage all around you. I honestly couldn't believe my eyes. I've never experienced anything like that in my life."

"I don't know what to say," I said. "I'm amazed."

"So was I," she answered. "Then when you returned to the minuet, the aura changed to a soft white before disappearing all together. I don't know what it all means, but I just wanted you to know that it left me wondering."

I could see and feel that the woman was physically shaking at this point. She wasn't crying or overwhelmed with emotion but was certainly affected. It was a moment that only we two shared—no one else can claim that memory except that lady and me. What an amazing gift was given to us both that evening.

All because I *"kept the channel open."*

God Stomping through the Sanctuary

Many times throughout my years serving as choirmaster and organist for various churches, I have heard God singing. Even though it is not uncommon for church musicians to regularly program, perform, conduct, and arrange the music themselves for all the services, I sometimes find myself on occasion actually listening as though I am part of the congregation.

As a result I discover that sometimes the music not only moves me but profoundly changes me, as well.

It is amazing still today that even though God can use musical servants as a channel for His song to others, there are times when they benefit more from the experience of being a conductor or performer than from those listening; simply because they allow the music (or the experience of the performance) to enter their soul and become a part of them—something that may not happen even during the most private of rehearsals.

One such moment was especially moving for me, and yet the experience didn't actually happen to me; it happened to someone else. While they were listening to the music I was playing, God was actually singing through me to them.

*   *   *

Each Sunday after worship I am fortunate enough to be greeted by various parishioners who wish to express their thoughts and feelings about the music offered at that morning's service. If you're a church organist you know that this can be a mixed blessing. "Oh! Your offertory was so beautiful this morning! It spoke to my heart. Thank you!"

Then there are the other times, "Why do you have to play so loudly?…and so *long*! I've got a roast in the oven and twelve people for lunch! Didn't you *know* that? What's the *matter* with you?"

Still, you take the good with the bad and continue on.

Once, though, just after I'd finished playing the postlude on a particular Sunday morning, a young gentleman I had never met before came up to the console and greeted me. He didn't introduce himself but asked if he could share a story. Since I was sure it didn't involve menus or turned-down hearing aids I pleasantly smiled and said, "Yes, of course."

Sadly, the gentleman began by telling the tragedy of how he had lost a close relative to a drunk driver several years ago. The following day after having received this devastating news he found himself in a very low place, and didn't know how he would be able to even make it through the day.

Gathering what little strength he could just to get out of bed, the gentleman did manage somehow to prepare for the day and drive himself to work. When he got there he just wanted to be alone, so he turned on the radio in hopes of easing his mind and finding some solace. Playing on the local classical music station that morning was *Appalachian Spring* by Aaron Copland.

Not thinking too much about God trying to reach out to him through this music, he just sat and listened. Suddenly, he was caught by the simplicity of its opening phrases. It was exactly what he needed—simplicity to ease his troubled mind. He began to describe the music to me.

"Tones," he said, "just tones. Nothing too involved. Peaceful almost. Then came that famous melody from the solo clarinet, *Simple Gifts*. As the piece went on and the variations become more intricate, my spirit began to lift. I realized through this music that life did indeed have everlasting hope, and I knew more than ever that God was never far from any of us in our time of need."

Amen, I thought to myself—but that wasn't all.

To further the story, the gentleman explained to me that he came to Immanuel Baptist on this particular morning only because the church he had planned to attend down the street was sharing their worship service with us.

What was so remarkable about this Sunday morning was that the very next evening this young man was to meet with the family of the relative who had been killed, and he didn't know just how he would be able to bring himself to see them once again after all these years. The feelings were still so strong in him that it seemed liked it happened only yesterday.

The gentleman admitted he had entered the sanctuary heavy-hearted and worrisome about meeting with the family. When it came time for the service to begin, however, he noticed almost immediately from reading the bulletin that the special music was the suite from *Appalachian Spring* by Copland. It nearly knocked him over!

Once again God was singing to him.

This gentleman found himself being directly ministered to through the same piece of music. But this time, he said, "I was ready for it."

Sitting there within the congregation, his eyes closed, tears streaming down his cheeks, a big, bright smile on his face, he received all that this music had to offer.

By the time the final triumphant statement of the theme came crashing down, tympani and all, he said he had a vision that "God was stomping through this sanctuary."

I was speechless. What an amazing image—what an incredible story.

"Anyway," he said, humbly, "I just wanted to come up and say thank you for playing that piece this morning. I felt as though you were playing it especially for me. God bless you."

…and with that, the gentleman simply shook my hand and quietly left.

Does God Sing?

* * *

As a person of faith, I realize just how fortunate I am that my life is blessed by experiences such as these and furthermore by the talents God has entrusted to me in order that I may forever be an instrument of His work.

But more importantly as a musician, I recognize that a church's sanctuary and service continually give me the opportunity and place to show God's love through music.

> Lord, make me a channel of your peace:
> Where there is hatred, may I bring love;
> Where there is wrong, may I bring the spirit of forgiveness;
> Where there is discord, may I bring harmony;
> Where there is error, may I bring truth;
> Where there is doubt, may I bring faith;
> Where there are shadows, may I bring light;
> Where there is sadness, may I bring joy.
>
> Lord, grant that I may seek to comfort rather than to be comforted;
> To understand, than to be understood;
> To love, than to be loved;
> For it is in giving that we receive,
> And it is in dying that we are born to eternal life.
>
> —Prayer of Saint Francis

Sing with Life!

Have you ever read the hymnal? Yes, *read* the hymnal. Not just sung the hymns' tunes merrily like that of a Sunday morning worship service but actually *read* the words as though you were reading a book of poetry? Try it—some of the most beautiful words of inspiration, hope, courage, support, and faith can be found in the words of the hymnal.

* * *

When I became an organist I was always learning from my observations of other organists. One in particular, the late Paul Havenstein II (one of the greatest organists I've ever known), used to baffle me beyond comprehension because whenever I heard him play I could never understand his musical interpretations of the hymns.

I had always approached my own practice time with a carefully calculated theory of arrangement that was entirely based within the musical structure of the hymn, but Paul would constantly throw in unexpected twists and turns that were so foreign to me that I wouldn't even sing—I would just stand and listen.

Afterward, I wanted to know everything he had done—and *why*.

"You mean, after all these years," he'd say with a smile, "you haven't figured out what I'm doing up there?"

"No," I admitted, "I'm sorry to say, I haven't…Will you teach me?"

"I can't teach you," he said, "but I can show you."

So he invited me to a private practice time during the week so that I could examine his technique. (Little did I know that his "technique" was anything but technical.) Still I went—eager to discover his secret.

I arrived at his church the following Tuesday morning at seven sharp—as instructed (he had already been practicing since four a.m.) and slipped quietly into the last pew in the back. Paul actually wasn't playing a hymn; he was practicing a tremendously impressive prelude that left me awestruck.

When he finished, he turned and said, "Oh good, you're here!"

"That was *incredible*!" I remarked.

"Oh, that old thing?" he waved away. "I've known that for ages. So…you want to know how to play hymns correctly?"

"No," I answered, "I want to play them like you."

"That's what I said." He laughed. "*Correctly.*"

"Correctly," I echoed.

"Okay then," he said, taking a hymnal from the pew and handing it to me. "Choose a hymn." I began to search.

As Paul made his way back to the organ console, he shouted, "But *not* your favorite! Something of substance!"

I thought for a moment as I thumbed the pages, and after dismissing many tunes, I finally settled upon a familiar standard that had, what I thought, musical substance, "Faith of our Fathers."

"'Faith of Our Fathers' it is," Paul said, taking the organist's hymnal, finding the number from the title in the index and turning to the hymn.

For several minutes I sat there and watched as he stared at the page. I couldn't understand this at all. What was taking him so long? *He must know this hymn by heart,* I thought to myself. *Is he actually studying the music? Is he arranging the music in his head—thinking up some incredible improvisational accompaniment? What?*

Finally, he declared, "Okay! Here we go!" and he began to play.

I sat and listened intently, following along as best I could, until once again Paul began to treat the music in a way that was unfamiliar to my ear. What was he doing? Why was he slowing down? What was happening with the upper register? Did he just completely *stop* in the middle of the line?

I waited patiently until he had finished even though I wanted to shout out, "What are you *doing?*"

After he ended, Paul turned around and asked, "Well? What did you think?"

"I have *no* idea!" I screamed in defeat. "I'm not getting it."

"Getting what?" he asked.

"What you're doing," I confessed.

"Well, it's actually very simple," he said. "Let me ask you—how would you play this hymn?"

I began to answer, but was cut off.

"No wait!" Paul exclaimed. "Let me guess. You state the first verse of the hymn as written—note for note. Right? And then on the second verse you let your choir sing in four-part harmony and back way down on the volume. Then, between the third and fourth verses, you improvise a bit and modulate up half a step. Am I right?"

He was.

"Ah!" he exclaimed. "But that's so...*English*!...And utterly *boring*!"

He jumped up from the console and ran down the aisle. "No, no, no, no, no...pick up the hymnal and turn to two-seventy-nine."

I did.

"Okay, now read the words," he told me.

"Out loud?" I asked.

"No...to yourself, stupid!" he replied. (He always had such a special charm) "Yes, out loud. Do it!"

So I began to read the words, "Faith of our Fathers living still in spite of dungeon, fire, and sword. Oh how our hearts beat high with joy..."

"*Stop!*" he cried. "Oh! That's *te*rrible! Just *te*rrible!"

Grabbing the hymnal from my hands, he sat down next to me. "Look." He pointed. "Look at the first words. It's not just 'Faith of our Fathers' but 'Faith of our Fathers!'—exclamation point! You see?"

"Yes?" I acknowledged, reluctantly.

"Well, then?" he said. "Play it! And here, read on. 'In spite of dungeon, fire, and *sword!*'" He raised his hand in a gesturing motion. "'Oh how our hearts *beat.*' You see? *Beat!* '...beat high with *joy!*'"

Waving his arms above his head, he raced back down the center aisle and took his place at the organ once again. "Listen!" he shouted back, and he proceeded to play exactly what he just read moments before.

Starting with a great statement of exclamation, he wielded a musical sword with that of a raging fire and beat out a heart in joy with his feet. I was getting it—the subtle pauses, the intense implication of meaning, the caressing of lyrical emotions.

He continued on, and I delighted in every word he *played*, wondering just what he would do next. The hymn came alive in a way that changed my way of reading a hymn forever.

"*Now* do you see?" he said, finishing the last triumphant chorus.

"Yes," I said, relieved. "I do."

"Good!" he exclaimed. "Now, your homework."

Homework? I thought. *What homework?*

"I want you to read the entire hymnal from the very first page to the very last and *listen* to every word that is printed. Translate it into music in your head," he said. "Ask yourself, 'How does one *play* love? How do you *play* praise?'"

That morning was one of the greatest life lessons ever taught to me. Paul Havenstein II went on to teach me so much more throughout his life, but for this one particular lesson I will forever be grateful to him.

* * *

I still teach this method of accompaniment today: "That is why a good organist will not *play* the tune but play the *words*. The words are the most important part of the hymn. They are the true soul and meaning of the hymn. Of course, we all identify with the melodies. It's the strongest memory reflex we have—the ability to recall a melody. Ask someone what their favorite hymn is, and if they name one because of its catchy tune, they're missing the point. But if they name a hymn and explain their reason for choosing based on what the words mean to them, then *that* is what a hymn is suppose to do. Read the hymnal like a book of poetry, and you'll allow any congregation to get the very most out of any hymn they sing."

For this reason, I would set before all, a charge to keep, take a hymnal home with you the next time you are at church—or ask to buy one. Every day read a hymn in the morning and one at night. A normal hymnal will take you a full year to finish if you read two hymns a day.

Try and sync it with the calendar year so you're not reading "Hark! The Herald Angels Sing" in the middle of June, and as hard as it may be *not* to sing the familiar tunes, just read the words. Like the scriptures, you will find great comfort and strength—since most were written at times of either trial and tribulation or the need to express joy and praise.

* * *

Now what is so remarkable about the hymnal is that even though we use it every Sunday morning, Sunday night, (even for Tuesday or Wednesday night "Hymn-Sings") in every church, very few worshippers actually know how to use a hymnal.

What are the strange names printed in the bottom right hand corner or (if you are using a *very* old hymnal) at the top of the page—in lieu of a hymn title? What do the metric-like numbers stand for? 8.6.8.6...10.11.10.11 refrain? Every hymnal is different—set up in its own format.

But what I find most interesting are the Methodist hymnals that include the famous (although, severely out-dated) "rules" for singing the hymns correctly by legendary hymn writer, John Wesley in 1761. Yes, *the* John Wesley.

- Learn these tunes before you learn any others; afterward learn as many as you please.

- Sing them exactly as they are printed here without altering or mending them at all, and if you have learned to sing them otherwise, unlearn it as soon as you can.

- Sing all. See that you join with the congregation as frequently as you can. Let not a single degree of weakness or weariness hinder you. If it is a cross to you, take it up, and you will find it a blessing.

- Sing lustily and with a good courage. Beware of singing as if you were half dead or half asleep but lift your voice with strength. Be no more afraid of your voice now nor more ashamed of its being heard than when you sung the songs of Satan.

- Sing modestly. Do not bawl, so as to be heard above or distinct from the rest of the congregation, that you may not destroy the harmony, but strive to unite your voices together, so as to make one clear melodious sound.

- Sing in time. Whatever time is sung be sure to keep with it. Do not run before nor stay behind it but attend close to the leading voices and move therewith as exactly as you can and take care not to sing too slowly. This drawling way naturally steals on all who are lazy, and it is high time to drive it out from us and sing all our tunes just as quick as we did at first.

- Above all sing spiritually. Have an eye to God in every word you sing. Aim at pleasing Him more than yourself or any other creature. In order to do this attend strictly to the sense of what you sing and see that your heart is not carried away with the sound but offered to God continually, so shall your singing be such as the Lord will approve here and reward you when he cometh in the clouds of heaven.

Does God Sing?

Whew! Somebody say, "Amen!" Those Wesley boys (Charles and John) really knew how to get a fire started—and keep it going! Where have the days gone when a fire was put in your belly?

They are humorous to read, but in reality, these "rules" are still used today. Although many versions stop after the first statement or sentence and leave the 'hell, fire, and brimstone' off, the message is still relevant.

We all certainly can name a particular choir or congregation member that fits one of those numbers. We may even chuckle upon reading the instructions and picture those certain "rule-breaking singers" in our minds. But if you study them carefully, you will find Wesley's true intent for setting forth such a list of rules. More importantly, there is a beauty in number seven.

* * *

While serving as organist for a Baptist Church, there was a lady in the congregation by the name of Ruthie Brown. God Bless her. She was a beautiful person. Although, one might, on first impression unfortunately, see her as being unkempt in appearance and even mistake her for being homeless. She had no teeth, wore tattered clothes, and spoke in an innocent, young-minded manner that might bring questions about her mental abilities.

But there was something very special about this lady. While others might pass her by entirely because she did not fit in with the upper class, encompass the finer standings of distinction, and did not communicate a higher sense of intelligence, there was a glow of honesty and kindness that surrounded her. She was a *good* person.

If I were to describe her in any way that would do justice to her character, I would have to say that she was probably as close to being a true Christian as one could imagine.

Her simple mind, her kind soul, and her pure qualities and quiet sense of being did not attract attention. Many did not even know her name. So for this lady to approach the director of music at a church that had a professional choir and highly respected music program and request to sing a solo was anything but customary. Even the most experienced of singers were rarely granted the opportunity to sing a solo. In fact, to allow any person from the congregation to sing on a Sunday morning during worship was something to be considered carefully, especially when considering someone like Ruthie Brown.

Could she even carry a tune? Was she capable of remembering the words? Would she just sing without any concept of what was coming out of her mouth? All of these questions came to mind when she approached me on a Sunday after worship.

As a professional organist and choir director who had been hired to keep a high level of standards for the music presented within the church, it was at times necessary for me to say no to the many requests that came to my attention through the music office. If God had not already spoken to my heart through this kind and gentle lady, I would have without a thought declined her request.

I asked her, "What would you like to sing?" (I honestly thought she would choose a child's hymn such as "Jesus Loves Me.")

But she replied, "He Touched Me."

This took me aback. "He Touched Me" was a beautiful Bill and Gloria Gaither classic—one that I had heard countless times during my youth in the Nazarene church. I hadn't heard it sung in years. Could I afford the risk of having her sing it—not knowing if she could even *sing*?

All this aside, I know from experience that when God wants you to hear Him, He does not let go. He does not give up. He speaks directly to your heart and says, "Open your eyes that you may see…"

So I said, "Ruthie, come into the church this week, and we will go through it together. I'll see you on Tuesday at ten a.m. sharp." (I had to give a specific day and time because in the past she was known for just not showing up.)

Not this time, however. Tuesday morning at ten a.m. there came a knock. Ruthie had arrived.

Keeping to my word, I asked her, "Now, you'd like to sing 'He Touched Me,' yes? Do you have the music?"

"No," she said, with a smile. "I don't need it. I know the words by heart."

"Do you have a certain key that you prefer to sing it in?" I questioned.

"No," she replied, confused. "I don't think so."

"Okay," I answered. "I'll play it in the key that it is written, and we'll see how it goes."

I knew that the key was far too high for her. She had a low speaking voice that did not carry much support behind it. I prepared myself for a very uncomfortable "audition," knowing that at the end I would have to politely decline her offer to sing in worship.

I began to play the introduction, which was merely the end of the chorus refrain, and *arpeggiated* the seventh chord, signifying that Ruthie should begin singing.

Ruthie did not sing—and so I stopped.

"Is everything okay?" I asked, "Do you need the words?"

"No," she said, smiling. "I'm okay."

I began again, *arpeggiated* the chord, and waited—still nothing. *Oh dear*, I thought, *this is not going to work*. So I nudged Ruthie into singing by prompting the first few words and playing the beginning notes of the melody.

Soon she understood that it was time to sing, and so she started...in the wrong key. I played steadily on, nonetheless, not wishing to stop and fix the problem. I realized it would be pointless to do so.

As she sang, she fumbled many of the words and lisped through the melody—barely maintaining the tempo. Before long she finished. Smiling a toothless grin, she looked innocently at me and waited for my response. I had no idea what to say; there were no words.

I said the first thing that came into my head, "Okay, Ruthie, we'll list it as an Offertory in a few weeks since the choir has already been programmed to sing the next three upcoming Sundays. But I have to ask...if I put this in the bulletin, will you show up and sing?"

"Oh, yes!" she exclaimed, "I'll be there!" And with that, it was set.

Weeks passed, and I did not see Ruthie in church. I began to worry. Should I submit the title in the bulletin and risk her not showing up? What should I do?

That voice once again said, "Open your heart," and so I did.

Sunday morning came, and as I was preparing to robe for the worship service, I saw Ruthie enter the church, smiling. She came right up to me and said, "I'm here."

"That's good, Ruthie," I said. "Now, here's the bulletin. See where it says 'Offertory'? That's when you will sing. I'll get up from the organ and sit at the piano. That's your signal to come forward and sing. Okay?"

"Yes." She nodded. "Okay."

Throughout the service I kept thinking, *What can I do to make this work? I can lower the key—that's not a problem. I'll relax the tempo and not double the melody—that's simple enough. I think if I just follow her, it will work.* I thought of a thousand different solutions to reassure myself that I had made the right choice in allowing her to sing.

Then I heard Paul say in the back of my mind, *Just play the words, stupid!*

And so the time came for Ruthie to sing. I made my way to the piano, caught her eye, and bowed my head that she should come forward.

As though she were a professional singer at Carnegie Hall, she walked down the aisle, turned, and stood directly in front of the entire congregation. She held her head high and smiled brighter than the noonday sun.

Before I could play a note, Ruthie looked toward the cathedral high ceiling of the church and said in a carrying voice, "This is for you, Mama." With those words, every heart opened—including my own—and there was complete silence.

I played the opening refrain and *arpeggiated* the same cueing chord. Before I could even think about repeating the opening or prompting her in any way, Ruthie began to sing—note perfect, every word pronounced clearly.

"Shackled by a heavy burden…'neath a load of guilt and shame…"

As she sang, with such absolute innocence and truth, Ruthie met every eye in the sanctuary. Each new phrase she sang, she sang directly to a different congregation member. At certain moments she would raise her hands to emphasize her deep faith.

By the time she reached, "He touched me, Oh, He touched me," I heard sobbing from the congregation.

When Ruthie spoke the words, "And *Oh!* The *joy* that floods my soul," she touched her heart; that's when I felt the tears stream down my own face.

The second verse brought forth more tears and weeping from the members of the church. Not once did Ruthie falter, nor did the smile leave her face. She met every eye and sang straight from her heart.

At the end, she repeated, "He touched me…" and looking up to the ceiling and finished with, "…and made me whole."

Does God Sing?

My face was soaking wet, and I barely found the strength to look out into the congregation. Many eyes were closed, several heads were bowed, and the hardest of men within the church were wiping their tears away.

Ruthie merely smiled, turned to me, bowed, and went back to her seat. She did not require applause or expect praise for her offering. It was not a part of her; it didn't even occur to her. This was absolute faith and complete surrender. To Ruthie, it was just God and her—we were just fortunate enough to be witness.

God sang to me that morning. God sang to every person in that sanctuary. Few things have humbled me so greatly as that one moment. It changed my life.

I don't know where Ruthie is today. I'm not even sure if she is still alive. After that Sunday I only saw her once more. She approached me before a service and presented me with an audio cassette tape (without a case) of gospel songs sung by Elvis. She wanted to sing one of the selections.

I never saw her again.

> Above all sing spiritually. Have an eye to God in every word you sing. Aim at pleasing Him more than yourself or any other creature...

Murodhon

While working as a choirmaster and organist at Immanuel Baptist Church in Portland, Maine, something happened to me that changed how I react to certain situations in my life not just musically but also spiritually.

One summer I received a call from an unknown lady who explained that she had been for the past year housing a foreign exchange student from Uzbekistan named Murodhon. She went on to explain that he was leaving for his home country the following week and had requested before he left to "see a real pipe organ."

She went on to say that he was very musical and played the piano himself and that I had been specifically recommended to her. "Would it be possible," she asked, "for us to set up a time for Murodhon to come and see the organ at Immanuel?"

Now, I have to admit, I was not looking forward to this. I was tired. It had been a very long church year, and I hadn't had much of a summer. On top of it all, I received at my music office several calls every day from people who needed something from me musically or personally, and before I had even met this lady, or this boy, I knew I was going to have to paint a fake smile on my face while I showed them the organ.

She was perfectly charming on the phone, and I'm sure the young man was very pleasant, but I was not in any mood to take an entire afternoon out of my busy schedule to show Immanuel's pipe organ to an unknown lady and her exchange student. Still, I did not let on my inner feelings, and scheduled a time for us to meet.

They arrived a few days later, and right away the young man, Murodhon, seemed very anxious, nervous almost, as his host mother and I talked about his stay and my job at the church. I thought perhaps he didn't understand English very well because his attention seemed fixed on something else while we talked, and his eyes were darting here and there around the church hallway.

Before long, I took him into the sanctuary, switched on the lights, and turned on the console—the very console I turned on every Sunday morning and each time I practiced. My eyes were unimpressed, but Murodhon's lit up. Also, my ears were used to the sound of the mighty blowers starting, but Murodhon's perked up.

I tried to explain as best I could from where we were seated how a pipe organ worked and pointed around the chancel throughout the introduction. But nothing could compare with what happened to Murodhon when I pulled a stop out and pressed a note. "Wow!" he shouted. (I thought he was going to jump off the organ bench!)

I asked him if he knew any pieces of music. He said, "Oh! I love *all* classical music! My favorite is *Toccata and Fugue* by Bach." I knew just what to do. I pulled on the full organ and played the opening bars of the Toccata for him. "Wow!" He jumped again! From that moment on, the smile that reached from one ear to the other never left his face.

I asked him if he could play the piece, and he said yes, he could. So I suggested he play it himself and that I would pull the stops around him and control the volume. He looked at his host mother as if to ask permission, and she nodded enthusiastically.

Murodhon touched the keys of a pipe organ for the first time, and his whole life changed. In his country, he later explained, there were no organs—of any kind. It was hard to even find a piano. Yet this remarkable young man had taught himself how to play and hungrily took in everything he could get his hands on. He reminded me of myself at that age and suddenly my afternoon didn't seem as pressed for time as before.

As he raced through the *Toccata*, I pointed to the different manuals he should switch to and continued to pull the stops for him. He could not play the pedal notes, so I assisted in that, too. When we reached the last final D-minor chord it was like the great gates of Heaven had opened up, and God Himself had granted Murodhon his one wish in life up to that point.

Later I took him up into the organ loft and showed him the inner workings. Every new fact he learned filled him with excitement. For the rest of the afternoon we played and chatted about nothing but music. Every piece Murodhon played he asked, "Do you know this?" and I would say, "Yes, that's by Chopin," (or some other composer) and his eyes would light up even brighter. Then I would play another work for him by the same composer. "Wow!" "Wow!" "Wow!" he exclaimed. (*Wow* was the word of the day.)

Soon, though, it was time for Murodhon to go. But before he left he asked if he could play the organ just one last time. I said yes, and he did. Afterward his host mother and I talked for a bit. All the while Murodhon stood affixed, staring back at the organ console as though he knew he may never see one again. Shortly I was waving good-bye to them both.

When they left, instead of returning to my office and attending once again to my work, I sat back down at the organ and just played piece after piece that I remembered learning when I first let music into my life. Pieces that I thought were boring since then and hadn't cared about or played in years—but through the eyes and ears of this young boy—became alive to me again. The hours ticked by, and I never did finish my work that day, but I didn't care…I was happy.

* * *

What I took away from that afternoon was feelings of guilt and humility and a little bit of shame. I had been given a great gift, a great talent, a great instrument, a great choir, a great job—and instead of greeting each day with the same appreciation and enthusiasm as Murodhon, I took for granted all that God had given me and complained about foolish, selfish things that didn't really matter. I filled up my days with so much complaint of chronic dissatisfaction that I tended to forget all the joys and blessings that I did have in my life.

Murodhon is back in Ubekistan now. I received an e-mail from him shortly after our meeting that contained lots of exclamation points in it. He wanted me to come and visit. He asked if I remembered when we played the "Tokkata and Fuge" [sic] on the organ. He said he talks with his parents about that day all the time.

To Murodhon this was something he would never forget, and yet he would only be allowed the memory of hearing and playing a pipe organ. To him, who has nothing, this is enough.

I have the pipe organ every day along with the memory. To me, who has everything, this is more than enough.

God sang to me that day through a young boy from across the world, and I heard Him. Then I realized, once again, He sings to me every day of my life, but I allow myself to wallow so much in my own selfish excuses—I'm tired, I'm too busy, I'm just not interested, I do enough already—that I am sometimes deaf to His song. He reaches out, but I rarely reach back.

* * *

This experience brings to mind a famous image—a painting.

I have a small photocopy of it taped to my computer screen so that I may see it every day before starting work. It's Michelangelo's masterpiece *The Creation of*

Adam. It is a remarkable work, but for me it carries an entirely different meaning from what many have been taught to observe: simply, God "breathing life" into His creation, Adam.

When you look at this painting, experts would have you see God on a magnificent bed of clouds, reaching down from the glorious Heavens, surrounded by several small angels—cherubs. Below lay Adam, limp and lifeless, extending one finger weakly toward God, humbly waiting for the divine touch of life. Yet, I have never seen this painting in this way. In fact, it poses just the opposite message to me.

I see Adam as being already alive. He is a strong, fully grown man who is lying lazily on the land. Not weak, but lazy—too lazy to even reach just one finger any higher than he already has in order to touch the very hand of God.

I can hear the excuses. What do you *want* from me? Haven't I given enough as it is? I'm tired. I've worked hard. On and on and on, we make excuses not to hear God singing—trying desperately to *reach us*.

And what does God do? Look closely. He's not just reaching down from Heaven, comfortable on a cloud, surrounded by his angels. No. He is leaning as far as he possibly can without falling, stretching out His mighty arm down to earth to try and reach Adam.

The cherubs? They are not merely accompanying God, they are holding fast to him so that he does not plummet in his attempt to touch Adam as if to say, "What are you *doing*? Come back! You're going to fall!"

Does God Sing?

* * *

Upon studying this painting further, I came across several analyses. God is depicted as an elderly, bearded man wrapped in a swirling cloak that he shares with some cherubim. His left arm is wrapped around a female figure, normally interpreted as Eve, who is not yet created and, figuratively, waits in heaven to be given an earthly form. God's right arm is outstretched to impart the spark of life from his own finger into that of Adam, whose left arm is extended in a pose mirroring God's. Famously, Adam's finger and God's finger are separated by a slight distance.

The composition is obviously artistic and not literal, as Adam is capable of reaching out to God even before he has actually been given life. Some scholars have even gone so far as to say that Michelangelo was inspired to paint this fresco in part from a medieval hymn, "Veni Creator Spiritus," which asks, "Finger of the paternal right hand (*digitus paternae dexterae*) to give the faithful speech, love, and strength."

* * *

God strains and stretches and reaches down to us, and we make every excuse possible in order to just lay back, propping our bodies on one arm, barely lifting ourselves up to the Almighty Himself—extending only one conditional finger.

This image is a reminder to me that every phone call I answer, every e-mail I read, every person I greet who walks through the door of my office, has a song to sing. It is our duty as Brothers and Sisters to listen to each other's song. He is reaching. Stand up, take His hand, and say, "Wow!"

His Eye Is on the Sparrow

When I was a boy of nine or ten, I was struck by a story of inspiration that was told in a sermon by a close friend of my parents.

Having been asked to share a message as guest preacher with our church one Sunday evening, he chose to speak about a hot summer's day, during a time in his life when he was at his lowest.

He had recently lost his job, his church and the congregation he faithfully served for nearly a decade. What's more, he felt that God had completely abandoned him and that his life held little value to Him or to anyone else, for that matter.

While driving down a long stretch of highway, he was lost in deep contemplation. For hours he had been wrestling with the disturbing feeling that nothing in his life was going right—that all the choices he had made so far for himself and his family were wrong.

Sweating from the heat, his lungs laboring for breath in the hot, stale air, he hardly noticed that his car was traveling at a dangerously high speed. It wouldn't have mattered even if he had noticed. His mind was racing faster than the car.

It was at this very moment that he felt a sharp, intense, striking pain in the middle of his chest.

In a panic, his first reaction was that he was having a heart attack. Being a man in his late fifties, heavy set, and under considerable stress, he could think of no other explanation.

"Dear God," he prayed, frantically, "don't take me now. I've got so much left to do."

As he pulled his car over to the side of the road, his thoughts instantly went to his wife and children, his relatives, and his friends. Shutting off the car, he put his head back, closed his eyes, and began breathing slowly and deeply.

Images of his two beautiful, young children flashed through his mind. Thoughts of his lovely wife and their lifetime of shared memories. Even their little poodle seemed to calm him. Soon his heart began to steady itself. His breathing came more easily. Although his shirt was still drenched with sweat, the light breeze coming in through the car windows cooled his body and his mind.

After a few moments, he opened his eyes and prepared to start the car. Looking down, he noticed that there, lying motionless in his lap, was a tiny, little, brown bird—a sparrow. It had been drawn in through the open window of the speeding car with tremendous force, shot into his chest, and died upon impact.

It was then that he knew that he was not alone and that God had a bigger plan for his life and was indeed

Does God Sing?

watching over him. Almost instantly he recalled the familiar passage from Matthew 10:29-31.

> Are not two sparrows sold for a penny? Yet not one of them will fall to the ground apart from the will of your Father in heaven. And even the very hairs of your head are all numbered. So don't be afraid–you are worth more than sparrows.

Keeping this scripture in mind, he placed the tiny bird on the seat next to him and continued on his journey. As he drove, he began to sing,

"His eye is on the sparrow, and I know He watches me..."

* * *

In 1904, Mrs. Civilla Martin was visiting with a sick friend, Mrs. Doolittle, who had become bedridden on account of a lifelong illness. During their conversation, Mrs. Martin asked the woman if she ever became disheartened because of her physical condition. Her friend replied, "Mrs. Martin, how can I be discouraged when my heavenly Father watches over each little sparrow and I know He loves and cares for me?"

Upon hearing these words, and while her sick friend rested, within just a few minutes Mrs. Civilla Martin wrote the words to one of the most inspirational songs ever written, "His Eye Is On the Sparrow."

Isn't it remarkable that God would choose the most common of all birds—sparrows of little value—to teach us such a profound truth? In God's eyes, no one is insignificant. No one is alone.

* * *

Obviously these two stories are unique. So unique, in fact, that it is nearly impossible for us to find similarities in their events enough to apply the message within our own lives.

Even when faced with insurmountable obstacles and personal difficulties, it is quite uncommon and certainly not an every day occurrence that a sparrow should fly in through the open window of our car in order to show us that God is always watching over us.

Likewise, few of us will ever find ourselves sitting beside a sick friend who, despite their physical ailments and failing condition, offers such divine words of peace and comfort that it should motivate us to write one of the greatest songs of hope. Yet we identify with the miracle of their revelations.

It is not unusual, however, in this day of easily accessible digital recordings that music should play such a distinct and present role in our lives in order to deliver God's song in a very direct and personal way.

I cannot begin to count the number of times I have been overwhelmed by emotion and burdened under the weight of unanswered questions about my life when at the very moment of almost giving up entirely a certain piece of music will suddenly appear and give me the courage enough to carry on.

Sometimes while driving in my car or at home listening to the radio, a song will enigmatically begin to play and completely change my outlook. Other times it may support my mood in a way that I no longer feel so alone. Often I draw just enough strength from the music to simply say, "It's okay to feel what I'm feeling…"

Music has the ability, more than any other art form, to combine restorative expression of the written word with the remedial connection to sound.

* * *

A close friend of mine, Dr. Peter Gray, once said to me, "Sometimes music helps me understand life better." Since this was a philosophy that I firmly believed in, I asked him what he meant. He told me this story.

"Some years ago I was working for a Social Service Agency. It was not uncommon, as part of my job, that when certain incidences occurred, the correct protocol required a written report to be completed and sent to the state's overseeing agency.

"One day a specific incident happened involving what was termed 'client-to-client behavior' and required just such a report to be filed. And so I completed one and sent it.

"At the same time I had been wondering if I would discipline the staff person involved any further than I had already, and this was on my mind when, shortly thereafter, a group from the state agency came and inquired about the incident.

"When asked what my plans were in regards to the client, I replied that I was sitting on it, meaning that I was still mulling it over in my mind about any further disciplinary action.

"The people asking me took this answer to mean that I had not reported the event. Before I even knew what was happening, they all left to decide what action *they* would take.

"The very next day, not only did the state's overseeing agency make the decision to suspend my agency's license to operate but found another agency to take over the operation, as well. I was immediately put on administrative leave so that my own agency could investigate.

"During this time I was worried that I would lose my job. I also felt confused by my own agency's actions and, what seemed to me, a lack of support. The hardest part for me was the overwhelming sense of helplessness that I felt toward trying to do anything to change the situation.

"In an attempt to explain what I had originally meant regarding my reply, I contacted the state agency. There was no response. Adding further to my feelings of helplessness was the fact that my own agency had taken me out of the picture completely by putting me on leave. I no longer had a voice in a situation that directly involved me.

"In a matter of days, it was concluded that I had done nothing wrong. However, due to the investigation process, it was discovered that there was actually no open supervisory position in the agency similar to the one I had previously held, and because the acting takeover agency didn't want to keep the existing supervisor—me—then I would be dismissed from my job. So I joined the ranks of the unemployed and began the dreary process of collecting benefits while looking for work.

"Some time later, only a matter of weeks, I believe, I was just by chance listening to one of my favorite singer-songwriters, Billy Joel. When I heard his song 'Say Good-Bye to Hollywood,' one of the lines in the song struck a chord in my heart. Instantly, what happened to me made absolute sense."

> Say a word out of line and you find
> That the friends you had are gone forever ...
> Life is a series of hellos and goodbyes
> I'm afraid it's time for goodbye again.
>
> —Billy Joel, *Turnstiles* (1976)

"So I said to myself, 'That's it. That's my story, too.' And along with that connection came some peace. Peace because I now could make sense of an event that before didn't make any sense at all.

"I continued collecting unemployment and looking for another job and kept in touch with family and friends for support. Yet even though I would get interviews and things seemed to go well, somehow I never got the position I was seeking.

"People would tell me, 'It wasn't meant to be—a better job is coming.' All I could say was, 'I hope so.' It's difficult to hear confident optimism when you're filled with subdued hope.

"Then one day it happened again. I heard another Billy Joel song, 'You're Only Human.' This time the words and music were inspiring me to hold on and hang in there. It really spoke to me and gave me energy—a lift.

> You've been keeping to yourself these days,
> Cause you're thinking everything's gone wrong;
> Sometimes you just want to lay down and die.
> That emotion can be so strong, but hold on
> Till that old second wind comes along.
>
> —Billy Joel

"You can see how this boosted my spirits and again described my situation. On account of it, I did find a job and things began to improve.

"After that I believed music could indeed add meaning to life and feed the soul. I still believe it. It can clear up confusion, it can inspire and instill hope, and because it is music…it gives life."

* * *

Years later I accompanied Peter when he decided to do something he'd wanted to do for a long, long time—sing a concert entirely on his own. He had planned to include both of these songs to illustrate how music gave meaning to his life and did sing "Say Good-Bye to Hollywood," but freely admits that he never quite got the hang of "You're Only Human" in time for the concert. So it was not performed.

"It's alright, it's alright," he said in his characteristically optimistic way, just like the song. "We all can't be Billy Joel, but sooner or later we'll feel that momentum kick in."

We're planning another concert…

Precious Lord, Take My Hand

John Philip Sousa once described how he composed...
Oddly enough, one might envision the composer of such rousing marches as *Stars and Stripes Forever* and *Washington Post* seated at a piano amidst a crowd of people, endlessly improvising melody after melody.

On the contrary, writing melodies was the hardest part of the composing process for the "March King." He even revealed once to a reporter the manner in which he would discover his most famous tunes.

Alone in his study, away from all extraneous distraction and noise, Sousa would sit for extended and often lengthy periods of time in complete and utter silence.

Almost as if he were in a state of meditation, with eyes closed, Sousa would force his mind to clear itself of all thought. In doing so, it allowed him to delve deep into the recesses of his subconscious where he would find the hidden melodies that made him so famous.

Some would say, the "quiet voice of God."

I know as a composer myself when I am in a place that is not of this world and spiritually inspired, I create works of music that I cannot explain from whence they came or how I was able to accomplish the writing. Many composers have related this similar experience.

When Johannes Brahms was asked how he "contacted God," the great German composer replied,

> That is a good question. It cannot be done merely by will power working through the conscious mind, which is an evolutionary product of the physical realm and perishes with the body. It can only be accomplished by the soul-powers within—the real ego that survives bodily death. Those powers are quiescent to the conscious mind unless illumined by Spirit. Now Jesus taught us that God is Spirit, and He also said, "I and the Father are one" (John 10:30).
>
> To realize that we are one with the Creator, as Beethoven did, is a wonderful and awe-inspiring experience. Very few human beings ever come into that realization, and that is why there are so few great composers or creative geniuses in any line of human endeavor. I always contemplate all this before coming to compose. This is the first step. When I feel the urge I begin by appealing directly to my Maker and I first ask Him the three most important questions pertaining to our life here in this world—whence, wherefore, whither (*woher, warum, wohin*)?
>
> I immediately feel vibrations that thrill my whole being. These are the Spirit illuminating the soul-power within, and in this exalted state I see clearly

what is obscure in my ordinary moods. Then I feel capable of drawing inspiration from above as Beethoven did. Above all, I realize at such moments the tremendous significance of Jesus's supreme revelation, "I and my Father are one." Those vibrations assume the forms of distinct mental images after I have formulated my desire and resolve in regard to what I want—namely, to be inspired so that I can compose something that will uplift and benefit humanity—something of permanent value.

Straightaway the ideas flow in upon me, directly from God, and not only do I see distinct themes in my mind's eye, but they are clothed in the right forms, harmonies, and orchestration. I have to be in a semi-trance condition to get such results—a condition when the conscious mind is in temporary abeyance and the subconscious is in control, for it is through the subconscious mind, which is a part of omnipotence, that the inspiration comes."

Who would have ever thought that the composer of *El Capitan* and the composer of *A German Requiem* would share such similar beliefs and yet come from two completely separate worlds and customs?

Similarities can be found in Patrick Kavanaugh's book *Spiritual Lives of the Great Composers* where he explores the inner light that inspired twenty of music's most prominent and well-known composers from the more likely such as Handel, Bach, and Beethoven to the less obvious Stravinsky and Messiaen, proving a simple fact that most men of genius, although different in character as their music, were all inspired by deeply spiritual convictions.

Likewise in poetry and song, the most inspirational words ever penned came from periods of time in many writers' lives when all hope seemed lost and they had given up on everything—even their own personal faith. Who could not be awestruck by God's ability to sing directly into the very hearts and souls of these writers and composers during such moments of complete despair and tragedy?

It's easy to find God when you're happy—but when you're hurting and in pain? That's when God finds you.

* * *

Thomas A. Dorsey's immortal "Precious Lord, Take My Hand" has been called the greatest gospel song of all time. People around the world know it, sing it, and love it because of its profound message of hope and faith. Written in 1932, it continues to appeal deeply to new generations of listeners. Though composed by a young African American blues pianist, the song crosses the lines of race and culture. Everyone from gospel legend Mahalia Jackson to rock 'n' roll king Elvis Presley has recorded it.

Like so many great hymns of faith, the song was inspired by a horrific tragedy in the life of its composer.

In 1925 Thomas A. Dorsey married Miss Nettie Harper. A year later, after experiencing some personal difficulty, he suffered a complete nervous breakdown that left him unable to work for nearly two full years.

Does God Sing?

To survive, Nettie was forced to take a job in a laundry in order to support them.

Seeking the advice of a family member, Dorsey was urged to attend a local church service. It was there that he experienced a spiritual awakening that healed him of his debilitating depression. Coupled with the sudden death of their young neighbor, the religious experience impelled Dorsey to devote himself more faithfully to God and sacred gospel music.

To mark the beginning of this new Christian way of living, Dorsey wrote his first gospel song, "If You See My Savior, Tell Him That You Saw Me," and in 1932 he accepted the position of choir director at Pilgrim Baptist Church in Chicago—a position he would hold for nearly forty years.

During his time of employment, the Great Depression took hold of America and its people. With their spirits waning, their hopes almost all but gone, Dorsey saw a ministry in his gospel song writing.

Dorsey once commented, "I felt my music lifted people out of the muck and mire of poverty and gave them hope." Sadly though, soon it would be Dorsey himself who would need spiritual lifting.

In late summer of 1932, Dorsey was billed as a guest soloist for a revival meeting in St. Louis. Pregnant with their first child and still living in Chicago, Nettie kissed her husband good-bye as he set off for St. Louis.

The following evening at the revival shortly after Dorsey had finished playing, a telegram was handed to him.

Dorsey recalls, "I ripped open the envelope and pasted on the yellow sheet were the words, 'Your wife just died.'"

Continuing, he describes an almost dreamlike moment, "People were happily singing and clapping around me, but I could hardly keep from crying out."

Without hesitation, Dorsey caught the next train home where he learned upon his return that Nettie had given birth to a boy.

"I swung between grief and joy," he confessed, "yet that night the baby died. I buried Nettie and our little boy together in the same casket."

Dorsey found himself at the very bottom once again, and even though he was able to muster what little strength he could to carry on through the funeral service, when it was all over he collapsed. He not only cut himself off from his family and friends, he even gave up on his music.

"I felt that God had done me an injustice," Dorsey said. "I didn't want to serve Him anymore or write gospel songs. I just wanted to go back to that jazz world I once knew so well."

But God would not let go, and in the depths of hopelessness and misery, Dorsey found himself alone in a small room with just a piano.

"It was quiet," he remembers, "the late evening sun crept through the curtained windows."

For the first time since hearing the news of his wife's death, Dorsey sat at a piano, and without any thought or purpose simply began to slowly run his fingers aimlessly over its keys.

Does God Sing?

Shortly, however, Dorsey would experience a personal revelation. "I felt at peace. I felt as though I could reach out and touch God. I found myself playing a melody, one I'd never heard or played before, and words came into my head—they just seemed to fall into place."

> Precious Lord, take my hand,
> Lead me on, let me stand,
> I am tired, I am weak, I am worn.

Here was a man who had started out his career known for leading a "sinner's life" as a blues piano player only to find God in the midst of tragedy. Transforming his life so completely that it allowed him to leave a legacy of faith and inspiration through hundreds and hundreds of gospel songs for generations to draw strength and hope from in times of struggle.

The life of Thomas A. Dorsey and his music was documented in the film *Say Amen, Somebody!*

* * *

In the film *The Color Purple* there is a scene close to the end where the character Shug (as in '*sugar*') Avery is singing jazz on a Sunday morning while her estranged father, a pastor, ministers to his church across the river.

Hearing her daughter singing this music, and knowing the lifestyle she has chosen that has separated her from the family and their faith, Shug's mother motions to her husband from within the congregation.

"Sing 'God's Tryin' to Tell You Something!'" she instructs him.

Quickly, whispers are heard among the parishioners. "Yes, sing 'God's Tryin' to Tell You Something'!"

Pastor Avery gives the word to the choir, and they begin to sing.

Meanwhile, across the river, Shug is still carrying on. "Let me tell you something, sister…" Suddenly she hears the strains of the familiar gospel hymn that she knows so well.

The music catches her so abruptly that she stops singing. Fighting the temptation to just listen, she attempts to return to her own jazz song—but to no avail. The music is so overwhelming and powerful it invokes deep emotional feelings within her.

"Yes, Lord," she hears, "If I was you, I'd say, 'Speak, Lord!' Speak to me!"

Shug sings in reply, "Speak to me…" In her heart she knows what she needs to do.

As she crosses the bridge, over the river toward the church, she continues to sing, "I love you, Lord! Save me!"

The sound of her voice as she draws nearer can now be heard within the church even over the choir and the young soloist who is singing the gospel hymn.

"Maybe God is tryin' to tell you something," she continues.

As the music bursts forth into a fast, gospel drive, the doors of the church are flung open. Shug Avery, accompanied by her entire jazz entourage, continues to sing full out, "I hear ya, Lord!"

Does God Sing?

Her father stands motionless in the pulpit, unable to take in the sight of his daughter, standing before him in his own church, professing her need for salvation and forgiveness.

Walking straight up to the pulpit, still singing, as the entire church is now caught up in the glory of the reunion, Shug shouts, "I'm gonna praise your name! Speak to me, Lord! God's tryin' to tell you something right now!"

His face wet with tears, Pastor Avery slowly takes off his glasses, makes his way down from the pulpit, and stands before his daughter. He does not move.

Shug quickly embraces him and whispers in his ear, "See, Daddy? Sinners have souls, too."

After a moment of her tight hold round him, he lifts his mighty arms up and takes hold of his daughter for the first time in as many years as he can remember. The choir continues to sing as father and daughter stand together at the front of the church in deep embrace.

> Lead me on to the light.
> Take my hand, precious Lord,
> Lead me home.

Crossing to the Other Side

> Music moves us and we know not why; we feel tears but cannot trace the source. Is it the language of some other state, born of its memory? For what can wake the soul's strong instinct like music? Nothing on Earth is so well suited to make the sad merry, the merry sad, to give courage to the despairing, to make the proud humble, to lessen hate, as music.
>
> —L.E. Landon

There is nothing I can claim from my personal culture, heritage, or even upbringing that would constitute a connection of any kind with the music for which I have become known for—ragtime, blues, gospel, and negro spirituals. Yet I have devoted nearly my entire musical life thus far to bridging the gap that has confined this music to a certain race, creed, or color.

I cannot explain it (Lord knows I've tried), but there is no definite link that I can find that would form such a strong bond between this style of music and me. Yet more than any other classified music, something deep inside me responds to its rhythms, its beat, its soul, its structure, its sound, its message, its form, and its essence. We are *worlds apart.*

In the musical *Big River: The Adventures of Huckleberry Finn* by William Hauptman and Roger Miller based on the novel by Mark Twain, the main character, a young boy named Huck, offers to help Jim, a run-away slave, reach freedom in the north. Even with a posse hot on their trail the two manage to find a raft and, climbing upon its back, get it afloat on the mighty Mississippi River.

Traveling only by night, the two don't get very far before they are reminded of the severity of their actions; a boat carrying captured runaway slaves ominously passes them in the darkness. As they remain motionless and silent, Huck and Jim hear the ghostly, rhythmic strains of "The Crossing," a gospel spiritual sung by people moving not towards but away from freedom. Although the sound is very familiar to the slave, Jim, it is quite foreign to the ignorant, naïve young boy's ears.

A slave woman sings in the distance, "Crossing to…"

"What is that?" Huck asks Jim, "You hear that?"

The young slave continues, "… the other side…"

"Slaves that tried to run off likes me," Jim replies, cautious and aware, "but they got caught. Now they's crossin' back."

"How you figure that?" Huck questions.

"I hears it in their singin'…" Jim replies.

"…We are pilgrims on a journey in the darkness of the night…"

Does God Sing?

All the while this spiritual is sung, an "overseer" in rhythm with the music calls out the order, "*Pull*."

* * *

When I first directed this musical, the preparation for staging this scene was simple. In fact, the notes found within the libretto could have supplied all that was necessary for any cast to perform the number. But something haunted me by this music—this scene.

Going against many of the conventional ways in which to stage this number, my production team and I added movement, sound, and visuals.

First, the visual—in silhouette behind a scrim, a large woman donned in traditional house servant, slave attire enters stage left and begins to cross, being heavy with burden. The audience does not grasp the reality of this "crossing," until the second direction is applied—sound.

As she sings the large slave woman leads with her left foot while dragging (in rhythm) her right—which is shackled to a chain. This segment of chain is linked to another slave…which is linked to another, and another, and another.

The third aspect (movement) is introduced by the commanding voice of an overseer crying out, "Pull!" With this one word, the chain is dragged one step at a time across the stage as the slaves reveal themselves, in silhouette, one by one, until the entire bound procession passes the raft and exits stage right just as the song ends.

Each night that number was performed, the theater fell silent. Not one breath could be heard—no movement of any kind. There was a deathly quiet that settled on the audience.

The dim lighting that barely illuminated the two fugitives in a faint blue light faded out completely as the first solo strains were called out by the slave woman.

"We are pilgrims—Pull! (*chain is dragged*)…on a journey—Pull! (*chain is dragged*) …" – and so on.

As the audience was submerged in darkness, and the soulful cry of the slave woman echoed throughout the theater, far in the distance the chorus of slaves began its rhythmic, thrusting hum against the cold, steel hauling.

When the spiritual reached its driving "call-and-response" before heading into the glorious joined refrain that spoke of Jesus reaching His hand, the cast was full on stage. The audience was no longer sitting in a theater in the late twentieth century; they were transported back to a time that allowed them no filter.

The shocking actuality of this sight, coupled with the singing and sounds created by the chain-linked slaves, was too much for even the most learned of minds to accept completely.

Although the musical production was filled with other spirited and intensely moving gospel, Negro and folk spirituals (many of which could reduce one to tears), "The Crossing" answered a voice deep inside of me that caused an indescribable sensation. I realized that I was not identifying with the characters in the scene but what the scene represented.

Here was a people, desperate to be free, knowing their own self-worth but not able to receive the respect due them, marching against the "Pull!" of authority and injustice all the while singing the hopeful, faith-driven words,

> I will worry 'bout tomorrow, when tomorrow comes in sight; Until then, Lord, I'm just a pilgrim crossing to the other side.

When we reach the other side, we shall all be equal. I asked myself, "Does this only apply to a specific oppressed race that suffered intolerable conditions during a definite time in history?"

If so, why then did I find my soul crying out in anguish when I first heard the soundtrack "Song of Survival" from the film *Paradise Road*? It completely destroyed me as did the *Holocaust Cantata: Songs from the Camps* when I first conducted the work. Why? How? I am not Jewish and did not suffer the Holocaust—nor was I ever a female prisoner in Sumatra during World War II.

It is a well-known fact that true, authentic Negro spirituals had hidden meanings in their words that even today can be traced to a metaphor of understanding. But at the time they were actually sung, the words were carefully chosen in such a way that hidden messages could be translated into valuable information that would lead escaping slaves to various "safe points" along their journey.

However, this cannot be said of "The Crossing" found in the musical *Big River*—a musical written entirely by a white composer, Roger Miller. This was the first connection I made with this music. It also raised the first important question in my quest to better understand and become an actual part of this music without the ability to claim ownership of its creation; did I need to be black, a descendent of slaves (a Holocaust survivor or prisoner of war), to identify with this music? The answer was and still is—no.

There may be endless arguments that arise from this one-word declaration, but I stand firm behind a lifelong determination based in discovery, study, and performance. The understanding is clear that there is no historical association that ties me to the field spirituals that were sung by working slaves, but no one can take away the direct bond I feel when I conduct a traditional gospel spiritual.

The association that I found early on with what were called Negro spirituals could only be established within the definition of overseer. The literal translation for this term is as follows—one who keeps watch over and directs the work of others.

What did this mean? Well, as history can attest, this definition has certain connotations that are far from any generalized description. In my mind the word evoked an image of a burly, aggressive, unyielding man on horseback with a whip who rode through the plantation fields and lashed at any slave that lagged in their work. Yet at the same time the variant of images stretch as far from the movie *Cool Hand Luke* as to that of the foreign film *Farewell My Concubine*.

These references did not diminish the severity I found in recalling oppression throughout history but served to equate a personal struggle that could be traced to each of us as humans. In other words...

Does God Sing?

Who were the overseers in my life? How did I assuage the feelings of having no voice—no identity? What supported and strengthened my self-worth in the face of dominating repression? From whence came my defense in times of trial and tribulation?

Faith and music.

I knew that I was able to conduct a Negro-spiritual "technically" correct—but it was the gospel spirituals that conducted *me*. When this happens, the true meaning of the musical term *spiritual* is realized to its fullest definition.

Historical research suggests that the origin of the actual word *spiritual* dates from the time 1275-1325 and is derivative from the Latin *spiritualis,* which is equivalent to *spiritu* (spirit). The definition for this one word has dozens of meanings. So how did I only know it as a song sung during the time of slavery?

I heard "Rise Up, Shepherd, and Follow" and "Go, Tell It on the Mountain" at Christmas time and pondered the hymnal when it read, "Negro Spiritual" (although other editions contained only the single word *spiritual*) Christmas? Negro spiritual? Where was the connection?

As a young man, I took it all for granted, accepted what I did not know, and enjoyed the music for what it was worth. It wasn't until I discovered Langston Hughes's *Black Nativity: A Gospel Song Play* that my *musical* world turned upside down.

* * *

In the mid 1990s, I was working for the music department at Bowdoin College. During this time I was fortunate enough to find myself accompanying the College Chorus under the direction of Dr. Anthony Antolini.

Tony and I became fast friends, and through our friendship he discovered that I was very much interested in a certain style of music, especially from America: early jazz, ragtime, gospel, and Negro spirituals.

One Christmas Tony came to me and said, "You know, Aaron, I have something quite special that I really think you'll enjoy."

Since I learned much of what were to be the early stepping-stones of my career as a choral conductor by observing this great man in action, of course I said, "Sure, what is it?" At which point he pulled out an old LP—it was the original cast recording of *Black Nativity*.

I had never heard of *Black Nativity* before, but trusting my mentor I went home and listened to it. The first song that I heard was "My Way Is Cloudy," and I instantly fell in love with this music.

I was riveted to that record player by the sounds that came pouring out of it. I must have listened to it nearly twenty times that very evening. The music grabbed me, shook me to my roots, and would not let me go. So I began to research.

This much I knew: on December 11, 1961, at the 41st Street Theater in New York City, backed up by only a piano and a B-3 Hammond Organ, six gospel singers made history. They performed *Black Nativity* by African-American poet Langston Hughes.

Hughes titled his creation a *Gospel-Song Play* because it combined traditional gospel spirituals with narration about the birth of Jesus. After only fifty performances on Broadway, *Black Nativity* closed. But there was a legacy—a rare recording.

That was it…

Even so I became consumed with this music and knew I wanted to perform it in some form. Perhaps not as the original *Gospel Song-Play* that Langston Hughes wrote but certainly in a concert version for the stage. So I went looking for the music, and I came up with nothing.

What quickly became obvious from my research was that Langston Hughes wrote this play called *Black Nativity* but accompanied his narrative text with a compilation of gospel spirituals that were already in the public domain to illustrate and carry the story of the Nativity.

So there was never any *printed* score written down—or at least published. The only thing that survived was that rare LP recording. So what I set out to do was simply transcribe one or two of these spirituals.

At that time I had a children's choir, and I wanted to perform just a few selections from *Black Nativity*. So I did: "Children, Go Where I Send Thee," "Rise Up, Shepherd, and Follow" and "If Anybody Asks You." But I also wanted to authentically recreate the sound I heard from that LP recording, and a children's choir would just not suffice. The spirit was certainly there, but the sound was definitely not.

Since there was no venue at that time that would allow a presentation of any kind to be realized and suited to my liking, I resigned to let my aspirations sit on the shelf for many years. Meanwhile, I developed other works for the concert stage such as Scott Joplin's opera *Treemonisha*—another work performed entirely by an all-black cast, written by a prominent black composer whose initial message was universal in its meaning (good versus evil), yet the production itself had very little to do with race except its setting.

It wasn't until I came to Immanuel Baptist Church in Portland, Maine, that the opportunity presented itself. There was something very special and unique about Immanuel. So open and inviting, it was a church steeped in tradition for performing every style of music imaginable (as long as it had a spiritual and communal message that all cultures could identify with)—there was no question that this was the perfect venue for a concert version of *Black Nativity*.

I was determined to say at long last, "This is it! We're going to do it!"

So after having listened to the album for years, I set to the task of creating a score with the firm belief that music is both universal and inclusive, encompassing no barriers of race, creed, or color. What's more, I offered the opportunity to perform in the premiere concert version to all those who were interested in singing a style of music that was not normally a part of their tradition.

The response was overwhelming.

Still, even with this musical green light, I did have to adopt a certain understanding from the very beginning.

Does God Sing?

That even though I myself might have "devoted most of my musical life to a style of music that was not my cultural heritage," others might not; and that together we would all have to learn how to allow this music to flow naturally, effortlessly, and, more importantly, correctly.

In addition, I realized it would be my duty to try to explain to those participating that acceptance goes both ways (or at least it should) when it comes to music that is now considered "universal." Universal in that several decades (even centuries in some cases) have passed, which has allowed a specific style of music to neither claim nationality nor culture enough that would limit its performance to an exclusive performer.

To support this I recalled that once in just one day I heard Andre Watts perform Liszt's *Sonata in B-minor*, watched Leontyne Price sing *Aida*, and downloaded a clip of Whoopie Goldberg perform the role of Pseudolus in *A Funny Thing Happened on the Way to the Forum*—and they were *fantastic*!

Andre Watts did not need to be Hungarian, Leontyne Price not Egyptian, and Whoopie certainly did *not* need to be a white, male actor to properly perform this music.

To further this claim, the very next day I purposefully located the following recordings and videos: William Bolcom performing rags by James Scott and Artie Mathews, Placido Domingo singing *Otello*, and Gunther Schuller conducting Scott Joplin's *Treemonisha*—and *they* were fantastic!

In theory, this philosophy sounded more than plausible; it sounded correct.

This was not the case, however, with those who had come forward to be a part of this premiere. Although their spirits were more than willing, it was rough going in the beginning, and much would have to be taught—and even more to be learned.

But can you teach how to authentically perform Negro and gospel spirituals? The answer is yes *and* no; one can recreate with some authenticity the "sound" of a Negro spiritual through applied technique and imitation, but one *cannot* teach the "spirit" of a gospel spiritual if the spirit does not personally shine from within; it has to come from a deep inner place that cannot be taught. It must be felt, believed, and lived.

One cannot force the spirit—the spirit forces you. Just like the Negro Spiritual states:

> I'm gonna sing when the spirit says sing,
> I'm gonna pray when the spirit says pray,
> I'm gonna moan when the spirit says moan,
> I'm gonna shout when the spirit says shout!

And obey the spirit of the Lord!

Most conductors know, though, that with choruses, if their spirits are willing, they can rise up to a certain level of aspired potential that can be found in all styles of music. So with the gospel spirituals, all that was needed in order to convey and transfer that aspiration to the audience effectively was the love of singing, the belief in the gospels, and the strength of the spirit.

Does God Sing?

Translating this philosophy correctly to what I had to work with at Immanuel may have been difficult—but it wasn't impossible. No, they were not a black chorus. They were not capable of creating a true a cappella African-American sound, because it just was not there. But that was not the point.

What *was* there and being produced was an infectious quality of life, an affirmation of the soul, and a joyful praise transferred from the soloist to the chorus to the audience. Through music, the spirit was passed. That's the live energy that comes out of this music. These spirituals are for everyone—*especially* the gospel spirituals.

But what of the "form" of these Negro spirituals—even the gospel spirituals sung at Christmastime? The form could not be denied its heritage. It was born from a direct lineage that incorporated the human voice, a strong syncopated beat, and more importantly, the call-and-response structure.

But what *is* a "call-and-response" spiritual? Actually, this is not a form found in just the black cultural heritage. It dates back to nearly all original cultures and 'religious' faiths. In the synagogue, the cantor would invoke, the people would respond; the Protestant church, the deacon would lead in verse, the congregation would sing the refrain; the Catholic faith, the priest would invite, those who were confirmed would come forward—and so on.

It is human nature; when asked, you either deny or respond. If you deny, you cannot sing. However, if you respond with supporting affirmation of your belief, you become a minister of music and begin to "preach" what you sing. "Go! Go, tell it on the mountain that Jesus Christ is *born!*" and usually, someone will shout from the audience, "Amen!" or "Hallelujah!"

Whether it's, "Shall we gather by the river?" the response is, "Yes! We'll gather by the river!"

"Have you got good religion?" The people shout, "Yes! We've got good religion!" And especially, as in the gospel Christmas spirituals such as "Wasn't that a Pity and a Shame," "If Anybody Asks You," and "Wasn't That a Mighty Day?" a statement is professed, and a response confessed.

In fact, I quickly realized that nearly all of the spirituals found in *Black Nativity* were gospel call-and-response spirituals. That was another very revealing truth in support that this music was indeed universal and was enough for me to conduct a sixty-five-member, white chorus with confidence and assurance.

So the process was half complete before we even started singing. They came because they believed. If you asked each of them, "Will you pass on over?" they would answer, "Yes! Lord!" They did not need to see it printed on the musical page; it came from within.

What transpired from the rehearsals for me personally, however, was the joy I received in witnessing the true and honest transformation that washed over each member of the chorus once they allowed themselves to shed all their inhibitions and just—*let go!*

I would explain to the choir every single time we rehearsed, "the soloist is calling *you,* and *you* need to respond with equal affirmation. A response of support for what the soloist is about to call out next—back and forth, back and forth—conveying and translating what the message is from that spiritual.

"If you are singing the same response over and over again, fifty times or more in one spiritual, and something does not change deep within your soul or if you become complacent and say, 'I've got to sing this *one more time*?' then something is not happening correctly. You need to continually change with this music so that you can always find something new in it."

There is something to say for the musical origins that came from this culture because the African Americans also invented the blues. And the blues is, as one knows, a low-down, gut wrenching, burden-filled style of music that by the end if you perform it correctly and really let go, you don't have the blues anymore—or at least you're not supposed to.

Just like the biblical scriptures from which these *gospel* spirituals draw their inspirational messages, a person can read the same verse over and over again throughout their life, yet with each reading one finds new meaning and on-going support to get them through even the toughest of times. That, in the words of one of my soloists, is the "glory of gospel music!"

During the rehearsal process, there was a chorus member who specifically kept e-mailing me and saying, "I just *love* singing this music because every time I do, something different happens. I bring something to it, or I hear something different every single time. Inside me, something changes. Nothing is the same. Nothing becomes stale."

Like the scriptures, the music never changes—*you* do.

For me, it was those first rehearsals that were so rewarding, but for everyone else, it was that premiere when we performed it for the public. Thinking back, I don't believe any of us knew what we had created until we performed it for the people in the audience who were going *wild* for this music.

The collective stomping, shouting, and clapping erupting from the audience was the one last essential element that truly made those gospel spirituals come alive. It was unbelievable, and we knew it. The moment we finished that first concert, we knew something special had happened and proved that, yes, it *does* go both ways.

We had crossed over and reached the other side.

The Tuning Fork

> The discovery of song and the creation of musical instruments both owed their origin to a human impulse which lies much deeper than conscious intention: the need for rhythm in life.
>
> —Richard Baker

The invention of many musical instruments began out of a simple human need and practical use. Ancient man, as they stretched animal hides in the sun for tanning, had only to take a stick and test its tightened readiness in order to learn that a resonating sound would occur. Place that prepared hide tightly over a pot of sorts, and one would discover the invention of the drum.

* * *

While attending the Boston Conservatory of Music, I was taught counterpoint by a professor who had what is defined in musical terms as—absolute pitch.

Now, nearly all of us have a "sense" of pitch. Meaning, if you can adequately sing "Happy Birthday" in tune with those singing around you then you have a sense of pitch.

Many are a step further and have what is called *relative pitch*, which is the ability to identify the intervals between any given tones, regardless of their relation to concert pitch (A = 440 Hz).

This isn't as difficult as it sounds. In fact, relative pitch can be acquired through properly applied ear training and developed with a bit of focused practice.

Most singers actually develop this skill on their own simply from years of experienced singing. It accompanies the fundamental and physical trait that most humans instinctively share—muscle memory.

The function of muscle memory allows one to know the exact feeling and placement at which a certain note will be produced within the throat enough to correctly sing a melody (following musical notation) by pitching each note according to its distance from the previous one—better known as *sight singing*.

In other words, place in front of a singer a piece of music that they've never seen before, give them a starting pitch, and they will sing what is written on the page.

Instrumentalists, on the other hand, develop abilities uniquely all their own, stemming from the same principles of practice and development but with the actual instrument of their training.

Position a trained concert pianist (classical or jazz) at the keyboard of a digital piano and, without telling them, transpose the key by electronic modulation. Ask them to play any piece of their own choosing, and they will instantly know that it is in the wrong key, even if it is within the difference of a mere half step.

More astonishing, though, is a tympani player—a really good tympani player.

My first real impression of just how skillfully honed the craft of a tympani player could be was when I had the great fortunate of conducting Leonard Bernstein's masterpiece *Candide* for orchestra and chorus. During rehearsal I witnessed this incredible sight.

Amidst the immense sounds being generated by a seventy-five-member chorus and orchestra at full volume, dozens of pitches, tones, and notes being produced with incredible vitality and strength that engulfed the concert hall, I looked over at the tympani player who was intently bent over her drums.

Placing her slightly opened mouth just centimeters away from the skin of the drum, she gently and quietly struck the tympani repeatedly while simultaneously adjusting the foot pedal until she had reached the next correct pitch. It looked as though she was kissing it.

It always fascinated me whenever she did this, and many times I would find myself watching her at certain moments when I should have been directing my attention to conducting because I knew that this brilliant percussionist was finding the correct pitch simply by *feeling* the vibrations with just her lips alone.

Side note (in case you were wondering): A 440 Hz simply means that sound waves being generated at 440 pulsations, or cycles, per second, will produce the note A. In fact, anything in nature that can create a rate cycle of 440 waves per second will cause a pitch to sound that of the note A. Vary the speed either faster or slower, and the note will become higher or lower.

It's like when we were children spinning those paper dragonflies with the rubber bands tied to a string. Remember those? The faster we spun them around our heads, the higher the hum became. HZ (hertz) is merely the unit of frequency equal to one cycle per second.

So technically if you were able to wave your arms around fast enough to cycle 440 times a second, you'd hear the note—A. Even the wings of a common housefly hum in the middle octave key of F.

But enough about the *mechanics of sound 101*; let's get back to the act of being able to distinguish pitches. We left off with *relative pitch*.

Even fewer of us are blessed with what is commonly known as *perfect pitch*. Sometimes *absolute pitch* and *perfect pitch* are defined as the same principle. But if one wishes to split hairs, there is a difference. A person with perfect pitch has the ability to sing any note asked of them without any musical assistance.

But a mere handful of human beings have the ability to name the precise pitch just by hearing a particular *sound*. For example, my former Conservatory professor. This ability is called *absolute pitch* and proves the scientific fact that anything that produces a sound wave actually produces a pitch.

During a class on four-part harmony, a fellow student accidentally pushed his chair backward, creating a sharp, scraping noise against the floor. Upon hearing this, our professor turned without hesitation and said, "F-sharp."

Does God Sing?

This caused a laugh among my classmates since many thought he was just being funny and had cracked a joke. To their surprise, he wasn't—and I was instantly fascinated by what was to happen next.

He proceeded over to the piano and played an F-sharp. Although he was correct, very few in the room were impressed enough to even realize what he had just done. It was at this moment in my life that I discovered I had talents blessed to me far greater than I had previously known existed—because I actually *heard* what he heard.

Although my skills would increase with experience over the years to a level that I could not even comprehend at the time of my Conservatory education, I have since realized that from the beginning the gift had already been given. It was a gift that could not be instilled or trained; it was already born inside of me—a gift that I can only describe as *God given*.

But still, for now, this was the question posed to the class, "How could a scraping chair produce an F-sharp?"

Many in the room were at least intrigued enough to join in the adventure, and so each began to test the professor. One student dropped his metal ruler onto the floor. "C-sharp," the professor said and supported his answer with the corresponding note on the piano.

Another student squeaked his sneaker sharply on the floor as if it were a basketball court. "A very high G..." came the reply. He was right again.

What our professor was showing us was that every object has the ability to produce a pitch. But most sounds found in our world are too brief in their existence and so do not register in our ears and minds as actual musical tones.

This same theory can be applied to the human voice. We actually "sing" every time we speak. But because our language includes consonants, the vowels are cut short and are not allowed to sustain long enough to sound a recognizable pitch that we associate with being musical in tone.

Our voices when we speak do not stay on a same monotone level. If it did, we would better hear the pitch being produced. Instead, our voices rise and fall, constantly moving from pitch to pitch at an alarmingly fast rate.

Some composers, such as Stephen Sondheim, have actually composed songs that are closer to human speech in their harmonic structure and musical inflection than that of a tuneful melody.

If we held on to our vowels within our words longer than what is required for normal speech, we would find ourselves generating a sustained musical tone or note. Even when we try and sing a consonant such as the letter T we are actually quickly passing the percussive *tuh* sound and straight to the vowel *Eee*.

I am forever telling my more *leaky* choirs, "You *cannot* sing an S! Sing *through* the vowel and *place* the consonant. One big vowel movement, folks! That's all I'm asking." I joke, "You're all too consonated!"

Just the same, have you ever noticed how one person's strangely pitched voice can grate on every nerve in your body? Relentless and annoying, and yet another's can be so calm and comforting to your ear that you could listen to them all day long?

It's because they are "speaking" in a particular range that resonates in our ears and also in our minds. Our bodies physically react to these vocal vibrations much like they react to musical tones. This is a powerful concept.

Is it a wonder that kidney stones can actually be broken into small pieces by high-energy sound waves adjusted to a particular frequency?

Music can be a very useful and effective healing treatment. (I'll save that for another chapter, though.) But our bodies do respond to music and can even define and regulate what music we listen to and enjoy. For example:

* * *

One day I was driving alone in my car, listening to the Mozart *Piano Concerto No. 20 in D-minor*. Submerged in the floating, delicate phrases of his celestial second movement, *Romance*, I was content to continue for the rest of the day completely lost in this musical world.

Then I found myself stopped at a red light.

While I was waiting for the light to turn green, another car pulled up in the lane next to me. The beautiful strains of the piano and strings that peacefully enveloped my entire body were quickly overtaken by an unbelievably earth-shattering, window-rattling, *Boom! Boom! Boom!* It sounded as though someone was dropping dump trucks in my head.

It was so blatantly loud that the Mozart was instantly overpowered and quickly disappeared entirely. The relentless pounding was literally causing the car and my body to shake as though a sonic boom was passing directly through my pelvis.

Boom! Boom! Boom!

Dear, God, I thought. *What is that noise!* I tried to locate the source.

Looking around, I quickly realized that it was coming from the very low-riding car, idling next to mine—its muffler rumbling just as loud as the music.

Since I was alone, no one saw my raised eyebrow and look of disgust, so I tried to make eye contact with the other driver. He was sitting low in the seat and off to the side—his left hand placed lazily at the wrist on top of the steering wheel. Eyes shielded by dark sunglasses, his head moved in rhythm with the music.

Then, to my surprise, I recognized the driver. It was one of my students from the university! Even though I didn't know it at the time, we were both headed for the same place.

The light turned green, however, before I could get his attention, and just as one would expect, the car shot off like a Nascar racer. It traveled so quickly that the mind-numbing thump of the music faded within seconds. Soon the noise, the car, and the driver were out of sight, while I unexpectedly found myself already into the third movement of the Mozart.

When I arrived at the university, I saw that the car was parked in the music school's lot. So I made it my mission to track the student down and ask him the one question that I think we all would like to ask the other driver when stopped next to their car, having to endure their blaring, head-thrashing music.

Searching the building, I found him on the third floor in one of the private practice rooms. Pounding on the door like his music was doing in my brain twenty minutes earlier, I smiled, he waved, and I entered—presenting the question.

"Man, how can you *listen* to that stuff?" I asked, "and why on *earth* do you have to play it so loud?"

I was shocked when I heard his response. "It relaxes me," he said, calmly.

"*Relaxes* you?" I repeated, stunned. "Are you *crazy*? How can that relax you?"

"I don't know," he shrugged. "It just does."

"Do you actually *like* that stuff, though?" I asked. "You're a classical violinist!"

"Yeah," he answered honestly. "I guess I do."

"Fair enough," I replied and went on my way.

Later, I pondered this answer for several days. I tried to wrap my mind around the whole situation. How on *earth* could anyone be relaxed by that music? If you could even *call* it music! (This was my personal reactionary judgment to the matter.) I just couldn't understand what anyone got out of listening to that noise.

But then I realized something: here I was a concert organist, and one of my life's pleasures was "pulling out all the stops" and just tearing into Charles Widor's *Organ Symphony No. 5*. Yet my best friend, with whom I share nearly every like and dislike, and is one of the greatest advocates for my music and talent, will not to this day attend a concert when I am performing just organ repertoire.

I remember very clearly her getting up during one of my first concerts after just a few selections and leaving. I met her for dinner later after the concert and asked her why she had left.

"I just couldn't take the noise anymore," she said. "My ears hurt."

"Your *ears* hurt?" I said, shaking my head. "How? This music is so powerful! Those magnificent thirty-twos in the pedal! … How could you *not* like it?"

"I didn't say I didn't like it," she said. "I said I couldn't take it."

"Couldn't take it?" I repeated, "Are you *crazy*?"

(As you can see, this is one of my favorite questions. I feel that by saying it to others it deflects all questions that could be directed toward my own sanity. So far, it has not worked.)

"I'm sorry," she continued. "When I hear the organ, my entire body tightens, and a sharp pain shoots straight up my spine and into my head. It feels like spikes in my ears."

At the time I couldn't understand this at all. I took it personally. *Ping*! Something struck deep inside, and I felt as though it was an attack on my music *and* me. We obviously did not share the same understanding and appreciation, so I just dismissed it with the belittling thought that she could not relate in the same appreciative manner as I did toward this music.

Then, while stopped at a red light several years later, it all came together.

Does God Sing?

When I produce a rumbling pedal passage using tremendous thirty-two-foot pipes, something reacts in my body, my gut, my chest—I *feel* this music. Music that could shake free kidney stones. It speaks to every fiber of my being. But it isn't the actual music that I am identifying with—it is the physical sound. It relaxes me.

It's not that my best friend didn't like this music; it's just that her body could not respond to it with any comfort or redeeming satisfaction. It did not speak to her because it never made it past the physical aspect of the actual tones and pitches produced by the organ.

Then I recognized that those continuous, pulsating *Boom! Boom! Booms!* that my student enjoyed listening to were not a reflection of his taste in music but more so how his body physically reacted and received them. It truly did relax him. So who was I to judge either him or my best friend?

But let's return to the basics: my professor and the understanding that everything creates a tone—a pitch. Unless it is allowed to sustain itself, it cannot reach its full potential of what we call a musical note.

So how can this applied knowledge—this sustained pitch—be effective in our lives? What does it matter if we sing when we speak or that a metal ruler dropped on the floor actually creates a musical tone?

It matters a great deal because God created all of this for a reason.

* * *

The most basic (and simplest) of all instruments in the world is the tuning fork—if it can be called a "musical instrument." What is a tuning fork? Wikipedia defines a tuning fork as:

> ... an acoustic resonator in the form of a two-pronged fork with the tines formed from a U-shaped bar of elastic metal (usually steel). It resonates at a specific constant pitch when set vibrating by striking it against a surface or with an object, and emits a pure musical tone after waiting a moment to allow some high overtones to die out. The pitch that a particular tuning fork generates depends on the length of the two prongs. Its main use is as a standard of pitch to tune other musical instruments.

(Trust me, this was the simplest definition I could find. All the others spoke in length about overtones, frequencies, and wavelengths.)

So, the tuning fork is a simple device that is used to produce the purest tone with which to tune an instrument. How hard could it be to use? You'd be surprised.

Most people handling a tuning fork for the first time, all seem to do the same thing. They take it by the handle, strike it against a table or chair, it emits a high pitched metallic *Ping*! (depending on its size), and they say, "Yeah? So?"

It's funny, but I had a coworker once who received a Tibetan Singing-Bowl as a Christmas present. She'd always wanted one because she heard they could produce beautiful sounds.

Does God Sing?

A Tibetan Singing-Bowl is a remarkable instrument that is handcrafted out of a single sheet of soft, thick metal and molded into the shape of a bowl. They range in size from ones that fit in the palm of your hand to others that are the size of a large cauldron.

Regardless of size, all are capable of producing one of the most hypnotically resonating and even eerie sounds in the world. If it is played correctly, the sound can almost cause your entire body to pulse along with its sound waves. However, in the hands of my coworker, it didn't come close.

It was some time after the New Year that she brought her prized gift into my office to show me. She proudly displayed it by saying, "I love these things!" and proceeded to strike all around the top of the bowl with the wooden pestle. *Ping—ping—ping!*

"Isn't that great?" she said with a smile.

I laughed, "Sure, but you're not using it correctly."

"What?" she answered in disbelief. "What are you talking about? Yes I am," and once again struck the top of the bowl several times. *Ping—ping—ping!*

"Give it to me," I said, and took the bowl. "Watch."

Striking it in a similar fashion around the top, I started the pitch sounding. But then gently began to rub around the rim with the smooth, wooden striker as though I was playing a glass harmonica.

It is the same technique one would apply if they were to run their finger over the wet rim of a crystal wine glass. You must continually administer a steady, equal, and firm contact in order for the glass to produce a tone.

Slowly a tone began to sound. Slightly at first but with a continued application of equal pressure rotating around the bowl, the sound grew increasingly stronger and louder. So much so that it was almost too intense to stand for very long.

"Wow!" I heard a voice call out from down the hall. "That sound is amazing! What is it?"

"Isn't that great?" I shouted back, "It's called a Ti—"

My coworker grabbed it from my hands, said, "Give me that!" and tried it again. *Ping!—Ping!—Ping!* and quickly turned the handle around and around the top of the bowl. But no tone was produced.

"Why isn't it working?" she asked, becoming more and more frustrated.

"You have to apply equal, steady pressure," I explained. "Try it again."

Ping—ping—ping—scrape—scrape—scrape, but again no tone was produced because the pitch was not allowed to sing properly.

"Slowly," I instructed. But it was no use.

"I give up!" she said and retreated quickly out of my office with the bowl.

"No, wait!" I offered. "I'll teach you!"

"Never mind!"

Slam! went the door to my studio.

Like the tuning fork, there is a life lesson in this story: whether a child or an adult, when a tuning fork is placed in unknowing hands, all that can be produced is a sharp, piercing—*Ping!*—and that is all. But there is more to this little device.

Does God Sing?

Almost like a magic trick, one must take the tuning fork (after all efforts have been exhausted), strike it on a hard object, point the tines upward, and place the handle firmly on a table or wooden box. It's only after striking the metal tines and the bottom of the handle is placed on a resonating chamber—open to receiving its tone—that one can actually hear a tuning fork sing.

When I am demonstrating this technique to children in a classroom, sometimes just for fun I will give them a task: to find something on which to place the tuning fork—and set forth the question, "Will it allow the fork to sing or not?"

"Quickly! Go!" I shout out to them. "But remember! It has to be something that will allow the tuning fork to sing!"

They scatter as if on an Easter egg hunt. Trying to find that one unusual object, outstanding and different from the rest, that will either stop the sound instantly or let it vibrate a tone the loudest.

One by one a variant of items are placed before me ranging from a rock to a coffee mug, a book to a shoe, a retainer case to a pencil box—all of which I let each child strike the tines and place the handle on to see if it works.

Some items allow the forks to vibrate throughout the room—others just ever so slightly. (In truth, everything has the potential to receive the sound. It's just a matter of volume and sustainability.)

It's all a matter of how "open" the object is to begin with that allows the fork to sing its sustained pitch the strongest and loudest.

It's after all attempts are through that I point out that none of them needed to go very far to find the perfect natural "receiving chamber" for the tuning fork to resonate its pitch. They quickly look around, trying to find what they had originally missed in their hunt.

So I ask for a volunteer. (Although confused, all hands shoot up instantly—not realizing that I will carry out a little "miracle" on one of them.) I choose a child at random to demonstrate and ask them to come forward. At which time I take out one of the biggest tuning forks I own. An audible gasp can be heard.

Telling the child to stand perfectly still, I strike the fork with such a tremendous force that it makes them all jump. Then I place it on the child's head, saying, "Now open your mouth"—and *voila!* The sound comes out.

A deep, slow, "*Whoa*," waves its way across the room, expressing wonderment and surprise. The volunteer child standing there with a tuning fork vibrating its pitch through his head can't help but smile through an open mouth.

"Close your mouth," I instruct, and the sound stops. This fascinates them. So to be fair, I allow each of them to come forward if they want to see what it feels like to have a tuning fork sound its pitch from the top of their heads. The one that creates the loudest tone, I joke, "Must have the emptiest head in class!"

It's a simple experiment based in natural theory, but I take the experiment even further by telling each of them the following. "Now," I say, becoming serious, "as odd as this may sound, pardon the pun (they never do because they never get it), but this is how I see life.

Does God Sing?

We are *all* tuning forks—either opened to resonating a beautiful song or closed to making nothing but a loud noise that gets us nowhere."

This is as far as I choose to take the analogy with the children. However, when I lecture to adults, I take it to the next level and introduce the most vital part of this statement—God. *We* are God's tuning fork.

God tries to "sing through us" each and every day of our lives. Some days are easy, others are more difficult, but we are all confronted with daily events in our lives that strike us like a tuning fork. Over and over again, something is always presenting itself—testing our "openness" to receiving God's true blessings – regardless of whether we see them at the time for what they are or not.

But my question is always this, "How do you react?"

* * *

I once worked with a Broadway producer whose answer to any suggestion or question presented to him, no matter how helpful or constructive, was always the same: "No." It didn't matter how pressing the issue, how insistent the situation called for a resolution, if anyone were to approach him with a useful solution or an idea, it was dismissed immediately without even the slightest thought of consideration.

"But you haven't even heard what I was about to say," comes the defense.

"It doesn't matter," he'd overrule. "The answer is still *no!*"

To those around him, such as myself who worked with him on a daily basis, this reaction was staggering to try to comprehend. It was simply unacceptable in our eyes. Instead of allowing others to offer their opinions and therefore perhaps even help in solving the crisis at hand, he would always choose to remain "right" and therefore allow the problem to persist.

However, we quickly became aware of this inevitable response and actually anticipated his veto. So we devised instead to subtly "offer" any helpful suggestions or constructive answers to what seemed to be an obvious solution (yet to him was an impossible obstacle to overcome) in such a way that it would seem as if he had come up with the idea himself.

Nine times out of ten, by simply walking away and leaving him to think on his own from the impetus seed that we had just secretively planted, he would emerge from his thought process and say, "Okay, so this is what we're going to do…"

By presenting our suggestions in just this sort of palatable manner, it allowed him to become open enough to "receive" the sounds that we were producing and thus solve the problem and move on. This method of transference of ideas worked without fail every time, but it was exhausting and, looking back on it, a complete waste of time and energy. What was the point?

There is a tremendous amount of energy produced when you strike a tuning fork; why waste it? Find a way to receive it and let it sing.

* * *

Does God Sing?

Like a struck tuning fork, what is your first initial reaction when faced with anything new or upsetting? Is it to instantly pull back and become defensive? Closed inside? Shutting out the world completely? *Ping!*

Perhaps come out of your corner with fists clenched ready to take on anyone and everyone who tries to oppose you? *Ping!* All the while making *yourself* feel as though nothing is within your control and no one is in agreement with you? *Ping!—Ping!—Ping!*

Even worse yet, when life strikes you—you, an instrument of God—when you're down as low as you can possibly get, and you feel as though the world just keeps kicking you and kicking you and kicking you—how do you respond?

Do you let out a loud noise?—erupting purely with raw emotion and irrational judgment that permits only you and your views to be heard? Allowing no room for any discussion, conversation, growth, healing, or understanding to take place within you, others, or the situation at hand?

This immediate reactionary response may allow you to be heard, but it also dies away almost instantly because even when you want to close up and run stomping off, screaming, "No! No! No!"—it is a short victory, one that places you further from any sensible reasoning or productive resolution with yourself (or anyone else, for that matter).

People may listen to you at the beginning, but after a while it grows tiresome. They begin to find it more and more difficult to listen, which in turn only causes you to become more closed and harder inside—like a rock.

God did not create us to become rocks. We were not born *rocks*. We were all born as resonating vessels of His love and understanding, always open to singing a pure, beautiful song as simple as that of a tuning fork.

If we just step back, allow the strike to happen, receive the blow but remain open, we find quite often that spiritual growth and better understanding can take place more easily. By letting ourselves be receptors to the situations that befall us, we allow acceptance and forgiveness, and better still, *faith* to become a part of the solution—faith in God, faith in those around us, and faith in ourselves.

Protestant minister and composer Rev. Alvin Allison "Al" Carmines, Jr., once preached,

> Faith is such a simple thing. It can't talk, but only sing. It can't reason, but can dance. Take a chance. Take a chance. Life is full of ways to go. Sun, rain, wind, and snow. All unknowingly we trace a geography of grace. From breath to breath and blink to blink, it's never quite the way we think.

So when something strikes you, remember the tuning fork; you can either react immediately or you can receive it, try and understand it, accept it, and therefore sing from it, through it, and even with it.

Sing unto the Lord a simple song...

* * *

Weeks later after the *Boom! Boom! Boom!* incident, I went back to the same student and asked, "Hey, just out of curiosity, what was the name of that piece you were listening to that day at the traffic light?"

"Oh, you mean 'Gangsta's Paradise'?" he answered.

"'Gangsta's Paradise'?" I laughed. "Are you serious? That's the title?"

"Yeah," he replied, "It's from the movie *Dangerous Minds*. You know, with Michelle Pfiefer?"

"Oh, yeah," I said, shocked, "I saw that movie. I actually liked it."

And so later that day I went out and purchased the soundtrack.

On my way home I played the CD in my car and listened to "Gangsta's Paradise." At first I just could not hear any redeeming qualities in this style of music. It was a driving, heavy, rhythmic rap, and I had long ago made up my mind that rap simply was not music.

But still, for now, I would give "Gangsta's Paradise" a chance.

I played the song again—still nothing. But by my third time listening, I slowly began to distinguish certain aspects of this music that I had not been able to notice due to my repellant fortress of disqualification set up years ago.

The connection I began to slowly make came in segments. First of all, the rap was not solely accompanied by a percussion track—there were full, rich strings pulsating actual chords on each beat. Chords that when I later took them to the piano found to be quite intriguing—based in the key of C-minor and passing through a series of fifths and fourths structured within the minor scale. *Fascinating,* I thought.

Then as I listened more closely by dissecting each element of the song, I was shocked to discover that the rapper was actually speaking on different pitches as though he was singing! (Many twentieth-century avant-garde composers such as Alban Berg and Arnold Schoenberg used this technique in several of their works, calling it *Sprechstimme*—meaning "spoken song.")

My God! I thought. *This is exactly what I've been looking for! He's actually speaking on pitch!*

When you listen to "Gangsta's Paradise," listen closely. The rapper, Coolio, starts out in a very low register of his voice and rises by major and minor seconds until he has completed a four-note series before repeating the pattern all over again.

Soon the soundtrack to *Dangerous Minds* became one of my favorite recordings. I listened to it all the time. I even found myself, while teaching a course on *Sprechstimme*, programming "Gangsta's Paradise" to demonstrate its use in today's world of modern music.

So since God has a terrific sense of humor, one day I found myself in my car, playing the soundtrack to *Dangerous Minds.* When I came to a stop light, I turned the music up full blast and let the force of those driving rhythms just wash over my body.

Looking over to the car stopped next to mine, I noticed an elderly lady looking at me with great disdain.

Does God Sing?

I smiled, rolled down the passenger's side window, and motioned for her to do the same.

When she had I shouted over to her, "I'm letting my tuning fork sing!"

The Healing Power of Music

Toward the end of Harold Arlen's life, although his musical legacy was by then set in history, Arlen's name was nearly all but completely forgotten. He was one of America's greatest songwriters, but much like his good friend, Harry Warren (another one of America's great *unknown* songwriters), he lived far longer than the era that recognized his genius would allow him the respect he deserved later in life. As a music historian, when I lecture on songwriters of the "Great American Songbook," I devote an entire series entitled *The Unsung Prophet in His Own Land*.

Unlike George Gershwin, Cole Porter, or Irving Berlin, Harold Arlen's songs were known in every household, yet his name was not. It's just the opposite with other "named" composers who people now acknowledge with celebrity status, but very few can actually name more than ten songs off the top of their heads.

With Harold Arlen, you could name dozens of his songs, and any person from one to ninety-two would recognize them well enough to sing their familiar melodies with ease. "It's Only a Paper Moon," "Get Happy," "I Love a Parade," "I've Got the World on a String," "Blues in the Night," "One for My Baby (And One More for the Road)," "Ac-Cent-Tchu-Ate the Positive," "Come Rain or Come Shine," "The Man That Got Away." Yet ask, "Who wrote that?" and the response is always:…???

* * *

In his book *Harold Arlen: Happy with the Blues,* Edward Jablonski writes this true but sad anecdote that occurred toward the end of Arlen's prolific yet unrecognized life.

One day, Harold was taking a taxicab ride crosstown in Manhattan.

> After he had settled in his seat, he found himself confronted by a classic situation. The cabby was whistling "Stormy Weather," an Arlen standard dating back to the thirties. It was an opportunity for experiment that the composer could not ignore.
>
> "Do you know who wrote that song?" he asked the driver.
>
> "Sure. Irving Berlin."
>
> "Wrong," Arlen informed him, "but I'll give you two more guesses."
>
> The cabby thought hard, and at times audibly if not understandably explained that the name of the composer was on the tip of his tongue, but he just couldn't come up with it.
>
> Arlen prompted him. "Richard Rodgers?"
>
> "That is the name I was thinking of," the cabby admitted, "but he's not the one."

Does God Sing?

"How about Cole Porter?"

"That's who!"

"No, you're wrong again," Arlen told him. "I wrote the song."

The cab darted across an intersection before the driver, still thinking, finally asked, "Who are you?"

"Harold Arlen."

At this the cabby turned around in his seat and asked, "Who?"

The same man whose classic "Somewhere over the Rainbow" was awarded the number one song of the twentieth century (yet his name was never mentioned in the press release stating the honor), had to live long enough to hear that one resounding word—"Who?"

"An unsung prophet in his own land..."

* * *

Our history is filled with unsung prophets. Many of which, sadly, are composers. To paraphrase another famous Jablonski quote, "If you want to be recognized as a composer, you either have to be European or dead—preferably both."

One such prophet, however, is one who when I mention his name will prompt you to turn around in your seat and ask, "Who?" Although, if I were to play the opening bars of *Mister Rogers' Neighborhood*, you would instantly recognize his style and genius and say, "Oh! Yes!" Yet there are few who know his name: Johnny Costa—one of the great jazz pianists of all time.

So why do we not know his name? This man should have been recorded in the annuls of musical history as one of the greats right next to Erroll Garner, Art Tatum, Dick Hyman, Thelonius Monk, *et al*, but he chose to remain "behind–the–scenes" for the great Fred Rogers for over thirty years.

These men are without a doubt two life heroes of mine who I have deeply admired ever since I was young enough to be enchanted by their magic and old enough to appreciate their genius…for one very simple reason; they let God sing through them. And because of this, they touched millions of lives. They sang what I like to call "God's Song."

One particular "song" that has never left my heart was one that I heard very early on in my career as a children's theater director. It is a hard story to come by since few know of this creative master of jazz music's life. The exact details have never been recorded to recall here; however, the beauty of the story is too great not to share.

During many appearances across the country, Johnny Costa would play, sometimes with his "neighborhood" trio, the familiar music that many children grew up listening to and knew well enough by heart to sing along. On special occasions, Johnny would ask a certain child to come up and sing one of his or her favorite *Mister Rogers' Neighborhood* songs.

On one such occasion Johnny asked for a young volunteer from the audience to join him on stage. As hundreds of hands shot up into the air, eagerly wishing to be chosen, a young girl raised her hand and caught Johnny's eye. He asked her to join him up on the platform.

When she finally made her way to the piano, Johnny realized that the little girl had Downs Syndrome. Asking what her favorite song was, she replied, "Silent Night."

Even though this song was not one from the show, Johnny smiled and said, "Silent Night. That is a wonderful, wonderful song."

As he played the opening, he turned to the little girl in an attempt to follow her every word. When she began to sing, he instantly discovered that she was tone deaf and not only couldn't sing in the key he was playing but could not even sing interval to interval adequate enough for anyone to even tell that the song was in fact "Silent Night," except for that of the words.

Johnny Costa was such a master jazz musician that with every note the little girl sang he modulated and constructed the most elaborate chords around each of her notes so that whatever she sang he made it sound right. So well did Johnny create an accompaniment for this little girl to sing her favorite song that he not only made her sound as though she was singing "Silent Night," but singing "Silent Night" perfectly.

At the end of her solo, the little girl received the greatest applause one could ever hope for after any performance. Because of Johnny Costa, no one even knew this little girl, who was challenged in so many ways, was completely tone deaf. All they heard was "Silent Night."

The audible applause was for her—the silent applause for Johnny could only be heard inside his heart. As Fred Rogers himself said of Costa and his music, "He is one of the most gifted musicians I've ever met. He is probably one of the finest jazz pianists in the world…with that kind of music, you [can't] help but find inside there, an exceedingly sensitive man. Which he is—a gifted, sensitive man."

What Costa did on stage that day was not merely pure genius but absolute unconditional giving—a giving that is born from the receiving, acceptance and acknowledgement of God's truest blessings and using them for the best and fullest of all possible good.

Because of this, Johnny Costa stayed for decades with the man children knew as Mister Rogers, playing his unique and brilliant piano stylings behind a camera that never revealed the source. Why? Well, as Johnny best explains it himself, he *believed* in what Fred Rogers did, stood for, and represented.

What Fred saw in Johnny, Johnny saw in Fred.

* * *

I truly believe that music has the ability to heal not only the heart but the soul and the physical body. I have not only heard but have witnessed the healing power of music.

Fred Rogers, an ordained Presbyterian minister, an advocate for the voice of children, an honored humanitarian, and even an accomplished songwriter, wrote a song entitled, "It's You I Like." In this song, as like many of Fred's compositions (he wrote all the songs for his children's show), a message is sung that was designed to make each child (and adult) feel special, unique, and worthy. But what is so beautiful about this scene is that a young boy in a wheelchair named Jeffrey Erlanger joins Fred in singing this song.

The scene from the original 1980 show was produced around the theme that some things can be fixed such as mechanical things—airplanes, cars, wheelchairs—while other things, such as bodies and divorces, cannot. Such was the case with young Jeffrey.

Jeffrey suffered from a disease that attacked his spinal cord and rendered him almost a complete paraplegic. His arms and neck were braced and jerked involuntarily. When he spoke, his small, frail body convulsed with each word. So when it came time to rehearse the scene, Fred uncharacteristically requested that there be no rehearsal and that they shoot directly to tape.

In the scene, Fred meets Jeffrey outside near the porch to his house. He asks many questions regarding Jeffrey's condition, his wheelchair, and his outlook on life. During this conversation, Fred unnoticeably shows his viewers that what makes Jeffrey unique is not his disability but the true beauty found deep inside that makes him so special. Because of this, Fred asks if he could sing the song "It's You I Like" to Jeffrey.

While Fred sings, "It's you I like, it's not the things you wear..." the young boy (who had been unable to control the movements of his body) begins to sing along. As he sings, his erratic movements, his uncontrollable twitches, slowly begin to lessen, and as the music progresses and the two sing together, the boy's body relaxes. His breathing regulates, and his body begins to respond to the singing and calm itself.

This is the healing power of music—and *this* is the gift of God working through a single man who saw the remarkable ability of this power.

> Not the things that hide you,
> Not your toys;
> (Fred changed the word "toys" to "fancy chair")
> They're just beside you.
> But it's you I like—
>
> —Fred M. Rogers (1970)

It is truly a miracle how music can pacify the corporeal body. It brings to mind the life of country singer Mel Tillis who developed a devastating stutter due to a childhood bout of malaria. It was almost a comic routine when he spoke, but when he sang, his stutter disappeared. Singing allowed him to conquer this lifelong impairment.

Then there is the heart-wrenching, tragic scene in *Hilary and Jackie*—the film depicting the life of famed cellist Jacqueline du Pre who suffered and ultimately died prematurely from multiple sclerosis. In a final scene, when Jackie's body reaches the irreversible stage that causes it to be seized with endless, overwhelming shaking, her sister Hilary holds her as one would cradle a baby and begins to sing a childhood song. Gradually, as her sister sings, Jacqueline du Pre's body responds to the peaceful music and ceases to shake.

Fred Rogers knew both the power of the written word and the power of the *sung* word. Because of this,

his life and philosophy touched and inspired children of all ages—as well as adults.

To know just how important each person was in his life, all one has to do is watch the television film footage that documents Rogers receiving the Television Academy Hall of Fame Award in 1999.

After a montage of clips from *Mister Rogers' Neighborhood* was presented in Heinz Hall, a surprise guest wheeled onto the stage to present Fred with the award—it was Jeffrey Erlanger.

In traditional Mr. Rogers' style, Fred (who was in his seventies) did not take to the stage by way of the stairs in a reserved manner; instead he leapt up out of his seat, scaled the front by jumping directly onto the stage, and ran to Jeffrey's side. In that auditorium of hundreds of people, only one person existed in Fred Rogers' eyes—the little boy he met some twenty years earlier: Jeffrey.

These stories touch our hearts in the same way the music that inspired them to touch our souls. We cannot escape or deny the effect they have on us. It is beyond our control. As a man, I cannot hear "It's You I Like" without crying, and as a musician, I cannot deny what I see when I watch that memorable scene between Mr. Rogers and Jeffrey—the healing power of music.

* * *

Few can argue that there is a direct connection with what can be considered both cerebral and emotional within these narratives—but where does the actual *physical* aspect enter into all this? Why did God create and envelop us with sound? Our hearts beat, but why in rhythm? It cannot be just to distribute blood.

Is it not a wonder of nature that by simply wrapping a ticking clock within a blanket and placing it near a restless pup, suffering from maternal separation, that it can be soothed to sleep by the muffled rhythmic beats replicating the sound and feel of its mother's heart?

If our souls can be healed by music, can our bodies?

The answer is yes.

In fact, today there are institutes that teach and train the physical healing elements that musical sound can produce.

During a studio class at the University of Southern Maine, voice teacher Ellen Chickering recalled to her students an extraordinary moment when she witnessed first hand how the human body could respond to musical sound. She remembered, "I was visiting the School for Functional Voice Training in Lichtenberg, Germany, with my friend Richard Conrad. He had attended this school for many years since going there in 1980 for voice rehabilitation after he was mugged in Boston.

"On this particular day, we were sitting in the garden area of the school, having lunch with Gisella Rhomert (the founder of the school) and Ruth Weimar, one of her teaching assistants, and some other folks. A gentleman came into the group and complained that he had a splitting headache. Ruth asked if she could do a little experiment. He said yes.

"So she got up from the table and, standing behind him, began to sing sustained tones into his vertebrae, starting at the base of his spine and moving up his back one vertebra at a time. It took about ten minutes or so.

"By the time she reached the top of his spine, she asked if he still had a headache, and he said no and looked quite surprised! Gisella took this as just another confirmation of the healing properties of sound."

* * *

The incomparable Leonard Bernstein (composer, conductor, pianist, historian, lecturer, activist, and musician), suffered greatly toward the end of his life from unbearable physical pain due to a lifelong addiction to smoking. In the last year of his life, he would confess, "Every time I take an inhaling breath, there is a sharp jabbing pain in my lower left lung."

The only relief he found, even more than that of prescribed medication, was while standing on the podium. Producing music, hour after hour, with a symphony orchestra, the suffering maestro hardly felt the stabbing pain that tortured his lungs.

"The only time that I do not feel pain," Bernstein told a friend, "is when I'm conducting."

But how could this be? Surely the demanding physical act of conducting would only exacerbate his condition and worsen the symptoms.

So we must question, could his mind have been so pre-occupied by all the various external stimulation and multi-tasks of having to direct a seventy-five-member ensemble that it was actually distracted from the pain? Could it have been the adrenaline surging through his veins from the sheer energy and excitement that blanketed his nerves and provided his body with partial sensory deprivation? Perhaps it was the endless flood of sound, flowing like a sea of waves from an entire symphony orchestra and pulsating through his body that in some way relieved his torment.

One might say it was all these elements combined: emotional invitation, intellectual capacity, and physical reception.

However, in order for the belief of this statement to be fully realized, one must follow it back to the beginning, complete the circle, and now ask the definitive question, "Can music heal the body *and* the soul?" Once again, Bernstein answers the question.

It would be noted that toward the end of his life, all the things Leonard Bernstein felt insufficient about (or those that would not or could not be realized) would at times be "taken out" on the music—released, so to speak—and very often he would stretch the music far beyond the limits of which it could reach almost to a breaking point.

Bernstein's final concert was given at Tanglewood, August 19, 1990. (He conducted his first major concert there and also his last.) Scheduled on the program was Beethoven's *Symphony No. 7 in A-Major*—a brilliant work of energy, vitality and force. If the event itself wasn't legendary enough, the Beethoven certainly was.

Nearly all the reviews at the time, and even those of today when referring to the recording, focus on the same observation—the tempos were unimaginably, almost painfully slow. Many critics were less than sympathetic to the fact that Bernstein was dying and could hardly lift his arms above his waist—reduced to expressing much of his direction through his eyes only.

But this was not the reason for the renowned maestro's carefully selected tempi. Nor could it fairly be said that the performance was simply a result of his failing condition. It was far more personal—it always was when it came to Bernstein.

His interpretations of many famous works revealed time and again throughout his life a deliberate choice to conduct them at slower tempos than those of which were not only traditionally accepted but also (if not more so) presently expected.

Whether it was Samuel Barber's *Adagio for Strings* (a work that conventionally called for an average playing time that ranged anywhere from six to eight minutes, yet under the baton of the great master was stretched to a staggering length of eleven minutes), or pulling the already impassioned, delicate musical thread that seemed to extend forever in Gustav Mahler's breathtaking *Adagietto* from his *Symphony No. 5* to a point that was nearly double in length of any other interpretation or recording to date, Bernstein seemed to achieve the impossible by wringing every last musical drop of emotion that could possibly be extracted from within these bars of music.

Even in 1989 while conducting the historic concert that celebrated the fall of the Berlin wall, Bernstein actually subdivided the heavenly strains of Beethoven's tender third movement (*Adagio molto e cantabile*) from his *Symphony No. 9 in D-Minor* and brought the eighth note down to a staggering *molto grave* and the sixteenth note to below sixty.

On a personal note, I remember that live concert vividly. It was well-known he was sick. One could clearly see, halfway through, how the physical strain from the first two movements had taken its toll on him—the second movement *Scherzo* in particular.

When that center camera zoomed in on Bernstein leaning back against the conductor's rail for support, and the whole world watched as he *did not move* for what seemed like an eternity, I thought, *Oh God, this is it. He's not going to make it.* But in true Bernstein form, after taking those long, deep, agonizing breaths to steady himself and regain his composure, he pushed forward, opened his eyes for just a moment to connect with the orchestra, closed them again, and began the third movement.

Sitting affixed to my television set, hardly breathing myself, I watched Bernstein gently extend his right arm out to indicate the half-beat; I thought it was the second beat! But he was actually *subdividing* the *Adagio*! I'd never heard it that slow. It was so slow, in fact, that it forced the first seat cello and concertmaster to conduct their sections (and cue each other) by large downbeats with their heads.

It was simply unbelievable to me. But slow as that tempo was, for Lenny, I truly believe at that moment, it was just Beethoven, the music, and himself. Nothing else existed. He was completely submerged in this music—wholly and utterly lost in its beauty.

Subjectivity aside, I also firmly believe that this music, at that tempo, was healing not only his body

Does God Sing?

but also his *soul*; he suffered from more than just physical pain.

It is understandable that Bernstein's bold choices caused certain controversy and even provoked numerous critics to label Bernstein as being self-indulgent. Yet today, ironically, most conductors and audiences consider his interpretations, such as the *Adagio for Strings* and Mahler's *Adagietto*, "standard" in their performances—acceptable, expected.

So in regards to the final concert and Beethoven's 7th, even though Bernstein conducted the famous *Allegretto* second movement more like an Adagio, almost a funeral march, close personal friends and relatives knew the reason why; he just didn't want to let go. He didn't want the music to end.

He didn't want the music to end.

As conductor Michael Tilson Thomas once revealed,

> [Bernstein's] music is intensely autobiographical. So the pieces do reflect [that constant] weighing of optimism and then concern… that all will somehow come out in the end—that there will be some kind of resolution and peace. That word—*peace*—was so important to him. When he talked about world peace, when he talked about music bringing you peace, or even the idea of a 'quiet place'—it was always that hope that somehow there would be a quiet sleep, a slumber in which there would be no nightmares…when he can smile and be proud of all that he has done.

* * *

My best friend for nearly twenty years (a brilliant artist and writer) has two daughters—Lindsey and Abby—whom I have had the great fortune and pleasure in watching grow from beautiful young girls into beautiful young women.

As adolescents, both girls were active within the Children's Theater, for which I was the artistic and musical director, and their mother was set designer for many of the productions. Before long, (due in part mainly to the fact that their parents had divorced when they were still at an early age) I "adopted" myself as somewhat of an older brother to Lindsey and Abby since much of our relationship was formed both inside and outside the theater walls.

For many years, in fact, we spent nearly every moment together. At one point I even lived with them. We shared many wonderful experiences. But the one link that joined us instantly and formed an almost unbreakable bond (even to this day) was *music*.

I wrote several pieces for the girls and would present them as Christmas gifts and birthday presents with proper dedications and performances while also introducing them to the different worlds of Broadway musicals, film scores, classical music, jazz, contemporary recordings, *et al*. I even taught little Abby piano.

Over the years as the two girls matured I took great pride in all their personal accomplishments and individual achievements. So when it came time for Lindsey to graduate high school, choose a direction for her life, and begin the selective process of finding a college, I could not have been prouder or more excited to learn that she wished to focus her studies on Expressive Art Therapy—an inspired profession that incorporates physical and emotional healing with the properties and power of art, music, dance, and drama.

Throughout her years of study, I was deeply invested in what Lindsey was learning and delighted in the exhilaration she felt at the wonder and awe of this unique type of therapy. In spite of the fact that it was still quite new in form, music therapy was (and is) an amazing treatment in all aspects of its practice.

It goes without saying that some of my fondest memories from those times shared with the girls and their mother were the discussions we had (many of which would last long into the evening) involving music, life, and healing.

Sometimes, though, at our happiest moments, the tragedies of life can strike hardest.

A few years later, just weeks after Lindsey received her Masters Degree from Lesley University in Cambridge, the girl's father suffered a sudden and severe heart attack; he was only fifty-five.

This is her story. "I had just said good-bye to the little girl I had been a nanny for—her name was Audrey. She was nineteen months old," Lindsey smiles fondly in remembering before turning serious. "Then I got a call from my cousin asking how my father was—this is how I found out. I didn't even know Daddy was in the hospital."

Just two days before, the girl's father, Wayne, had gone in for a routine medical test with his local doctor. From there he was issued a stress test at a larger facility, Midcoast Medical Center. As a result, it was discovered that his heart had almost complete blockage.

Wayne was seen as a strong, powerful, resilient man—a fighter. Even so, the following morning he was directly admitted to Maine Medical for an emergency quadruple by-pass surgery.

In such procedures involving coronary artery bypass surgery, a portion of a healthy vessel (either an artery or vein) from the leg, chest, or arm is used to create a detour or bypass around the blocked portion. In this case, the vein was taken from the leg.

Consequently, the leg contracted a severe infection. (An infection that strikes a mere 1 percent of all patients undergoing by-pass surgery and prevents all blood flow within the limb from occurring) In addition, significant bleeding was discovered around the heart, and a second procedure was immediately ordered. Subsequently, Wayne fell into a coma.

By this time, two hours—but a whole world—away, Lindsey had frantically notified her mother back home, quickly picked up her sister, and was fast on her way driving speedily up to Maine.

"It's strange," Lindsey remembers. "In all the years I was at school in Cambridge, I never kept my car down there with me. For some reason that week I had my car."

To others, this minor detail of circumstance might go unnoticed, but Lindsey relates this particular coincidence with a sense of pondering connection.

Upon hearing this, I am instantly reminded of the spiritual "Angels Watching over Me."

> We pray for those who long in pain,
> Angels watching over me, my Lord;
>
> Pray for strength to carry on,
> Angels watching over me, my Lord.

Angels aside, before the girls were able to reach their father, the second operation had taken place. Wayne now lay unconscious in his hospital bed—still no pulse could be found in his leg,

"No reason could be found by any of the doctors," Lindsey states, "It was seen as a complete mystery."

It is said that prayer is a constant—faith a necessity—but sometimes even the strongest of faiths and the most reverent of prayers have difficulty in providing the much needed comfort and assurance during such trials.

Nevertheless, Lindsey approached the attending male nurse—someone who would prove to be a continuous support (*angels watching over me, my Lord* ...)—and asked, "I have my iPod with me. Would it be alright if I go and get it so that he can listen?"

This simple question was met with understanding and sincere compassion—permission was given.

"I believed Daddy was scared," Lindsey remembers.

And so, employing the knowledge she had acquired from her years of study, armed with an applied practice of wisdom and a firm belief, Lindsey resolved to try and make her father as comfortable as possible by way of letting him listen to his favorite musician: Van Morrison. It was her instinct to do this.

She asked the male nurse, "Will he be able to hear this?" There was a definite assurance and even a positive re-enforcement of optimism. That's all that Lindsey needed to know.

Placing the listening phones in her father's ears, Lindsey, with her sister Abby, stayed by his side, playing the songs of Van Morrison.

From the moment Lindsey brought her iPod into the hospital room, the music never stopped.

Song after song, hour after hour, the girls at times took turns listening to the music with their Dad, placing one earphone in his ear, while they listened with the other—sharing the experience.

I asked Lindsey once if she remembered listening to specific songs during this time that would be of significant meaning in hearing them today. Oddly enough, she remembers the songs her father listened to alone more so than the songs they listened to together.

The music was a form of connection that linked the two together—it was in the moment, a present bond that now is not remembered for its particular details, but more, the sharing of the experience itself.

Although Wayne was visibly unresponsive to the music, something astonishing happened physically within his body. The male nurse on duty made the remarkable discovery; a pulse was actually found, and the blood was beginning to flow back into the leg!

Amazingly, the facts were undeniable—the leg was slowly coming back to life, and the blockage was no longer there. Some might call this a miracle—divine intervention even, but I believe that Lindsey had actually administered the physical healing power of music on the human body—her father's body. Her music therapy had worked when all medical attempts had failed. The therapeutic response to sound was greater than that of the response to medicinal treatment. It was a tremendous moment.

But with all storms, there is a brief flash of peace and calm just before the real lasting devastation occurs.

Even though the mood was optimistic enough for the doctor to tell Lindsey, "It's okay for you to leave. He's stable enough for you to do what you need to do." By this time the girls had been staying in the room since their arrival—curled up in chairs. In as many hours as it would take for Lindsey to drive down to Boston, quickly gather a change of clothes, feed her pets, and race back to Portland, upon her return, she discovered that her father had taken a turn for the worse.

His kidneys started to fail, the blood stopped flowing through his leg again, and his vital organs began to shut down systematically at an alarming rate. For the first time, the music stopped playing.

Lindsey remembers, "There were so many tubes going in and out of Daddy, people all around, coming in and out, it just wasn't possible."

All efforts were now focused on just keeping Wayne alive. Although no one ever said, "He's dying. He's going to die," it was just understood.

Friends and family had begun saying their goodbyes. One by one, those who had come together were slowly departing until Lindsey and Abby were left alone.

Their father was suffering now. His body was dying; he was dying. The male nurse who had been with the girls throughout could tell what was happening. He informed the girls, "I'm going to start unplugging machines now."

"He told us that," Lindsey realized, "because he knew as Daddy's organs began to shut down, the machines would start making noises. I think he was trying to make what was happening less traumatic for Abby and me."

In the final hours, sensing her father was suffering and in pain, Lindsey knew what to do—but this time it would be different. It would not be for relief…but for release. Release was all she could give her father at this time.

While he lay dying in his bed, Lindsey gently slipped the earphones back over her father's head so that he could hear once more the music she had brought especially for him.

"It was a way of passing," Lindsey signifies, "to leave that hospital…that body…this life."

There in the stillness of a quiet hospital room my best friend's daughters, remarkable young women, lay by their father's side, watching him listen to the music that had given him such great joy throughout his life.

Sometime after midnight, the heart monitor went flat line—"Daddy was gone."

* * *

Does God Sing?

In reliving these moments, Lindsey pauses, (thinking in retrospect to all the weeks, the months, the years that would follow) and says, "Now, listening to Van Morrison today, to this day, it keeps Daddy alive for both Abby and me. I am so scared that something will happen to [Van] because if he dies, it will be as though Daddy was dying all over again. He and his music meant that much to Daddy—and now to me and Abby."

The very next day Lindsey drove back down to Boston with her best friend and packed up her entire apartment in one night. They never said one word.

"There were a lot of good-byes that week…a lot of good-byes."

*   *   *

> "Everyone should have his personal sounds to listen for—sounds that will make him exhilarated and alive or quiet and calm."
>
> —Pierre Boulez

The Song of the Crane

I spent most of my years growing up surrounded by endless fields, deep woods, and sweeping open skies. Thinking back now, it was very much the life one reads about in books or watches on television and film.

Although I read Laura Ingalls Wilder and Louisa May Alcott as a child, studied Henry David Thoreau and the writings of Scott and Helen Nearing in high school, and even reveled in the life of a simple country vet tending farm animals in the hills and shires of England on public television, I never related those stories and the beauty of nature they vividly portrayed with my own life.

Yet there we were, my sister and I, at the edge of the great field, skating on the little pond that rested in the valley just below the hill on which we would sled during the short, winter days. The brilliant, reflective blue filling our darkened house at night from the full moon that illuminated the open winter sky with a brilliant, shimmering white across the fields of icy snow.

The crisp, clean air of autumn with its cold, brittle snaps of brightly colored leaves crunching under foot while voyaging through the woods on great adventures yielded a smell of fall so pure and good that grown men would weep upon taking it into their lungs.

Soft dew alighting the newly spun webs strewn across the fresh cut lawn in the sparkling green, spring-filled morning sun; while memories were born from seeing the far-off surrounding high hills glowing with deep, rich, orange-reds in the black of night as they were burned in preparation for the next year's blueberry harvest.

One cannot imagine how beautiful it was to breathe the cool night of summer with all its fragrance of newly mown hay, the mist arising off the still, quiet lakes, and trees breathing in rest from the long hot day, or how serene, listening to the woodland birds calling their individual evening songs as the small marsh frogs blanketed the fields with continuous sound.

The warm breeze of summer wafting gently through my bedroom window; I fell asleep each night to the sound of a whippoorwill singing its nightly song from its nest just below the sill.

Looking back now, I realize how fortunate we were to grow up in such beautiful surroundings. Now that I'm an adult, however, it's quite ironic that most people who know me associate my lifestyle with one personal quote, "I don't do nature."

Pity. It's these memories that I miss most out of any other time in my life, but one in particular stands out in my mind as having the greatest impact.

Does God Sing?

Each year, the three fields that stretched across our land just in front of the house were allowed to grow long throughout the summer months in order for them to be ready for haying in late August.

A week or so before we were to start school again, the familiar sounds of heavy machinery would begin rumbling from far below the second pasture and make its way laboriously up through the great field. The tractors, with their massive wheels as high as a horse, hauled behind them haying machines that shredded everything in their path with colossal, spinning, auger-like blades.

Normally I looked forward to this annual cutting and would marvel at the sheer mechanics of watching the tall grass be cut, thrown high into the air through the giant blowers, and strewn into the flattened path behind.

This year however, the tractors came early, and I was not there to see the haying. Instead, I returned home to a completely leveled field. All three had been mown. As I stood gazing out our large picture window over the open land, I noticed something strange.

Directly in the middle of the field there stood a small, brown, thin bird—a sandhill crane. I watched it closely, wondering what it was doing there amidst all the hay.

At first I thought that it was searching for meadow snakes or field mice that had been shaken from their burrows by the earth reverberating under the constant pounding of the engines. Then I imagined it was merely resting on its long migration flight to other lands.

Before I could think of another reason, the reality hit me with a sickening feeling in the pit of my stomach.

With one long, soulful cry, I realized that this young crane had built her nest in the middle of our great field. She had been scared off by the noise from the approaching threshing machines, and when she returned, the nest and her chicks were gone—destroyed.

As I watched, the young mother crane did not move from the spot. She did not look around, searching. Perhaps that was before I came home. Now she just stood there, not raising even a foot, calling out a song, a mother's song…a song of loss.

This beautiful bird stretched her long, graceful body to full length and pointed her head straight up in an exquisite line with her beak opened wide to the heavens. The sound that this creature emitted rose from the very bottom of her lungs, pushing her breast out with great force, and vibrated the muscles violently up through her elongated neck.

It was a sad, mournful, wailing cry.

Unlike the comforting vesper calls that most lake birds produce with light, reassuring vibrato to one another, this was a sole, sustained song that started with a low, deep tone without waver then rose slowly to a high-pitched keen that broke off, echoing into the dead summer air.

This beautiful, young mother crane knew nothing of the ways of man. She could not comprehend haying machines or balers. She did not know that there even existed a house from which a young boy stood

Does God Sing?

watching her through the large picture window just a few hundred yards away.

All that she knew came from one instinctual feeling of utter sadness and loss. She was in mourning. She did not know of logical thought or the laws of man. What did it matter if within the house from which the boy watched there were televisions and radios, electricity, and plumbing, bills to be paid, meals to prepare?

She just knew that she felt, and therefore—cried. She cried until the sun began to set. She cried long after the boy could no longer stand to listen. She cried out in song.

A song that no symphony orchestra nor chorus, no songwriter nor composer, shall ever be able to perform or compose that could move me as deeply and as purely as the song I heard that late summer's eve from a young, mourning crane that had just lost her children.

It made my world seem very small—and made God's world very, very big.

> Keep two pieces of paper in your pockets at all times.
> One that says, "I am a speck of dust."
> And the other, "The world was created for me."
> —Rabbi Bunim of P'Shishka

The Poetry of the Earth

> For the beauty of the earth, for the glory of the skies, for the love which from our birth over and around us lies.
>
> —Folliott S. Pierpoint

Leonard Bernstein, in his famous series *The Unanswered Question—Six Talks at Harvard* began his sixth and final lecture with a poem by John Keats which proclaims that the "poetry of the earth is ceasing never."

Within this one poem of divine beauty, Keats describes all the birds, hiding in the cool trees, singing, while the grasshopper takes his rightful place amidst the summer sun and brings forth his own distinctive song with great delight. Even the cricket when the frost has settled in on a silent winter's night, shrills his song near a warm stove.

In such picturesque and lyrical description, Keats almost defies us not to hear the sounds that surround us at all times: the sounds of nature—the earth.

A lovely image—a sentimental notion—but what does it mean?

* * *

Few people realize that we are always enveloped in song. When I say "song," I am not referring to the conventional songs we hear on the radio or those that can be found on a CD—tempered musical notes and syncopated rhythms—but more the actual pitches and tones that are generated from every object and organism found on this planet.

Popular American lyricist Moss Hart writes, "Music is there in the cycles of the seasons, in the migrations of the birds and animals, in the fruiting and withering of plants."

Take for instance *The Song of the Reed* by the great poet Mowlana Jalaluddin Rumi. "Listen to the story told by the reed—'Since I was cut from the reed bed, I have made this crying sound'—The sound it makes is for everyone."

It is said that after cutting reeds from the side of a river bed and the remaining stalks of the reeds are dried and hollow at the tip that the wind blowing across the open tops of these reeds produce a whistling cry, a tone, a note, thus giving birth to the modern day flute.

Can you imagine the beauty of experiencing such a phenomenon? Standing beside a river with the warm gentle breezes blowing softly across the waters—brushing the broken tops of the reeds, a symphony of mellow, flute-like tones filling the night air. This is a kind of music that can fill your soul unlike any other.

Does God Sing?

But the reed needs to be open in order to produce its song. And so, within the same poem, Rumi takes this image a step further with a profound message:

> Days full of wanting, let them go by without worrying that they do.
> Stay where you are inside such a pure, hollow note.
> Every thirst gets satisfied...
> [for those] who swim a vast ocean of grace ...
> no one lives in that without being nourished every day.
> But [not] if someone doesn't want to hear the song of the reed flute ...

This same message can also be found in the scriptures; it is God who has given us the gift of music. They who have ears let them hear. We are like children sitting in the marketplaces and calling out to others,

> "We played the flute for you, and you did not dance; we sang a song, and you did not mourn" (Matthew 11:17).

* * *

Since the invention of musical notation, composers have sought inspiration from the sounds they heard around them. Ludwig van Beethoven heard the poetry of the earth on many of his famous nature walks—*The Pastoral Symphony*. It is even said that he gained inspiration for the rhythmic and flowing third movement of his brilliant *Piano Sonata No. 17 in D-minor*, (*The Tempest*) simply by watching the natural gallop of a horse.

Antonio Vivaldi recreated the memories he experienced within the beauty of each season while serving as *maestro di violino* at the *Conservatorio dell'Ospedale della* Pietà in Venice—*The Four Seasons*. (If you ever have the opportunity, try and obtain a physical copy of the musical score to this masterpiece. You'll find within its pages that Vivaldi actually writes a programmed description for each segment. Although the main reason for its creation was originally intended simply for the amusement of his students, the music was inspired by nature and has been associated with it ever since.)

Even George Gershwin heard his own kind of poetry of the earth while riding a noisy train from New York to Boston in the early 1920s—*Rhapsody in Blue* and composer Ferde Grofe (who first arranged the Gershwin classic) later went on to write one of the most recognized nature-inspired works of all time—the *Grand Canyon Suite*.

The story goes that Ferde Grofe found himself at the canyon in 1916 and arrived in complete darkness, being unaware of what lay just beyond his campsite. The following morning he was awakened at sunrise by nature coming to life. "I could not describe the beauty of it in words," he explained, "because words would be inadequate." Instead, Grofe captured what he felt and saw in sound.

Years later in an attempt to explain why he thought people responded so deeply to his Suite, Grofe quoted his father who saw a "wide range of emotional possibilities" in the Grand Canyon. Sunrise evoked a feeling of birth, for example, while a cloudburst brought forth both feelings of death and resurrection.

> We were made to enjoy music, to enjoy a beautiful sunset, to enjoy looking at the billows of the sea and to be thrilled with a rose that is bedecked with dew...Human beings are actually created for the transcendent, for the sublime, for the beautiful, for the truthful... and all of us are given the task of trying to make this world a little more hospitable to these beautiful things.
>
> —Desmond Tutu

Even in the world of today's modern film score, a composer can create the most incredible piece of music by merely watching the elegant stride of a whooping crane—as can be heard (and seen) in Bruno Coulais's setting *Return of the Cranes* from the documentary *Winged Migration*.

Everything, even a train, creates its own sound—its own rhythm—its own song.

* * *

Leonard Bernstein ended his *Six Talks at Harvard* with this brilliant passage—a musical creed of sorts.

> I also believe, along with Keats, that the poetry of earth is never dead as long as spring succeeds winter and man is there to perceive it. I believe that from that earth emerges a musical poetry,

which is by the nature of its sources tonal. I believe that these sources cause to exist a phonology of music, which evolves from the universal known as the harmonic series and that there is an equally universal musical syntax, which can be codified and structured in terms of symmetry and repetition.

[I believe] that by metaphorical operation there can be devised particular musical languages that have surface structures noticeably remote from their basic origins, but which can be strikingly expressive as long as they retain their roots in earth.

I believe that our deepest affective responses to these particular languages are innate ones, but do not preclude additional responses which are conditioned or learned; and that all particular languages bear on one another, and combine into always new idioms, perceptible to human beings.

[I believe] that ultimately these idioms can all merge into a speech universal enough to be accessible to all mankind; and that the expressive distinctions among these idioms depend ultimately on the dignity and passion of the individual creative voice.

What an amazing testament. A little heavy in its wording, and certainly deeply intent in its meaning, but it definitely sums up his musical beliefs—and in the process defines even more.

* * *

Does God Sing?

In his Introduction to *The Sacred Journey* Frederick Buechner writes, "The swallows, the rooster, the workmen, all with their elusive rhythms, their harmonies, and disharmonies and counterpoint became, as I listened, the sound of my own life speaking to me. Never had I heard just such a coming together of sounds before, and it is unlikely that I will ever hear them in just the same combination again. Their music was unique and unrepeatable and beyond describing in its freshness. I have no clear idea what the sounds meant or what my life was telling me. What does the song of a swallow mean? What is the muffled sound of a hammer trying to tell? And yet I listened to those sounds and listened with something more than just my hearing; I was moved by their inexpressible eloquence and suggestiveness by the sense I had that they were a music rising up out of the mystery of not just my life but of life itself. In much the same way, that is what I mean by saying that God speaks into or out of the thick of our days."

This, I believe, is the poetry of the earth that Keats was writing about—and music plays a very important part of this belief. Music surrounds us—even in the simplest and most natural of places; you just have to be open to hearing it.

Katharine Hepburn lived by a personal family motto:

Listen to the song of life.

Epilogue

In the beginning was the note, and the note
was with God.

And whosoever can reach for that note,

Reach high and bring it back to us

On Earth to our earthly ears,

He is a composer,

And to the extent of his reach,

Partakes of the divine.

—Leonard Bernstein

Bibliography

De Mille, Agnes. *Dance to the Piper*. Atlantic-Little, Brown Books. 1952

Joel, Billy. "Say Good-bye to Hollywood." Album: *Turnstiles*. Family Productions/Columbia. 1976

Joel, Billy. "You're Only Human." National Committee for Youth Suicide Prevention. 1985

Abell, Arthur. *Talks With the Great Composers*. Citadel Press. 1998

Walker, Alice. *The Color Purple*. Film by Steven Spielberg. Amblin Entertainment, Guber-Peters Company, Warner Bros Pictures. 1985

Miller, Roger (Music & Lyrics) and Hauptman, William (Book). *Big River—The Musical*. Grove Press Publishers and R&H Theatricals. 1982

Jablonski, Edward. *Happy With the Blues*. Da Capo Press. 1988

Roger, Fred. *It's You I Like*. Copyright © 1970

Thomas, Michael Tilson. *Leonard Bernstein—Reaching For the Note*. Written and directed by Susan Lacy and produced for the series American Master by WNET, New York for the Educational Broadcast Corp. 1998

Bernstein, Leonard. *Findings*. Simon & Schuster. New York. 1982

Buechner, Frederick. *The Sacred Journey*. Harper Collins Publisher Inc. 1982

CPSIA information can be obtained at www.ICGtesting.com
Printed in the USA
LVOW07s1603130514

385613LV00001B/256/P